# Designing Your

# Life

*Unlocking the*

*infinite possibilities of the*

*subconscious mind*

Dennis M. Postema

Second edition: March 2014

# Contents

# Introduction:
# Is It Possible to Have It All?

There's a question that seems to be on everyone's mind these days: "Is it really possible to have it all?" While most recently this has been asked in reference to working mothers, everyone—regardless of gender, marital or parental status—wants to know whether they can actually reach all their goals and see each of their dreams come true. My answer is yes.

You might wonder how I can be so sure that you—and everyone else—can have it all. Just like you, I've dealt with my fair share of adversity on the road to realizing my dreams. The struggles I've faced have ranged from the loss of my dream job, a diagnosis of ulcerative colitis, a disease that causes an inflammation of the large intestine. I've dealt with multiple surgeries, the rebuilding of my colon, an almost fatal medical incident just after my wedding, and some major hiccups during my first book release. I've stood at that precipice where it seems everything is going wrong and you've already reached your peak, the weight of that invisible ceiling of maximum potential pressing down on your shoulders.

However, I refused to allow the ceiling to limit my potential. By learning how to harness the power inside, I converted the ceiling into a roadblock, and then found a way around it. Each time I did, I moved onto the next stage of my life and grabbed the next brass ring.

I'm not the only one who can have it all. You can too. All you need to do is stop roaming around in the dark with no direction. It's time to reach for your goals—and achieve them. You are the only person who can attain your dreams. It's up to you, and you alone, to create the reality you want.

Yes, you can be rich. You can be successful. You can be loved. Those goals that seem to lie beyond your grasp aren't unreachable. They're there for the taking. You just need to be willing to engage your creative mind, and start building the future you deserve. It starts with believing this important fact: *you are better than your conscious mind realizes.*

Have you ever allowed yourself to think about the possibilities before you? Too many people are so terrified of dreaming about what they can achieve, they actually get in their own way. If you're one of those people, relax. This book will change the way you think and the way you act. How? It will teach you to use a simple, decade-old technique to steer the course of the conscious mind through the subconscious mind.

No, this is not some silly, wasteful method offering little, if any, real insight. It's a proven technique used by thousands of people over decades, people who've had great success. This method can help you strengthen your mental powers, cast out self-doubt sabotaging your success, help you build an optimistic outlook, give you courage and confidence, and help you bring out your hidden talents.

Before you finish this book, you'll have practical methods to:

- Listen to your real self and uncover your true goals in life. It doesn't matter what others think or say; you have the answers for your own life's path buried within your mind. All you need are the skills necessary to unearth them.

- Get acquainted with your true self and recognize your hidden talents.

- Find the confidence to succeed. Successful people exude positive energy. Once you know how to tap into that energy, you'll find success is much easier to attain.

- Learn exactly what you need to do to achieve your dreams. Each of us has the ability to pave our own path with our words, thoughts and actions. The difference between those who succeed and those who fail is the ability to develop and follow that path.

*Designing Your Life* is more than a self-help program. It's a business book, a motivational book, a book on healthy living and even a psychology book. Within its pages are the secrets you need to get what you want out of life. Whether you're after money, influence, respect, love or all of the above, *you can have it all!*

# One: Prepare to Design Your Own Reality

Reality is subject to interpretation. What one person perceives to be the "reality of the situation" may not be how another person sees it at all. Just watch an afternoon of courtroom television and you'll see how two people can remember and interpret a situation in remarkably different ways. Listen to two separate sides of any argument to see how each individual's perception of reality colors their response and mood.

If reality is open to interpretation, it's also open to creation. That's right. We can each create our own reality. Your mind doesn't work as a result of what your body does—your mind is full of energy that propels your physical body forward.

There are two levels of the mind on which you should focus:

1. The conscious

2. The subconscious

## *The Conscious Mind*

The conscious mind takes in impressions through the senses (sight, hearing, touch, taste and smell) to make all the daily decisions that keep your life on a forward trajectory. Anytime you perform a conscious act, such as picking up a pencil, speaking to a waiter or making a phone call, your conscious mind sends orders to your body. When you turn in for the night, your conscious mind goes to sleep.

## The Subconscious Mind

The subconscious mind, on the other hand, never sleeps. It literally keeps you alive. If it weren't for the subconscious mind, also referred to as the unconscious, your heart would stop beating, your lungs wouldn't take in oxygen and your other involuntary functions would cease to work properly. In no time at all, you would die.

The subconscious mind is also responsible for governing your personality, your character, your inner drives and your deepest and most secret desires. It's also the seat of your creative mind, which holds the power to make you anything you want to be. The creative mind is responsible for taking an ordinary person and making them extraordinary.

J.K. Rowling is a great example of someone who used her creative mind to attain her dreams. The famed author of the well-known Harry Potter series began roughing out the idea for her famous stories on a napkin while waiting for a delayed train. At that time, she was an unemployed single mother on welfare. She wrote her first novel, *Harry Potter and the Sorcerer's Stone,* but she had a difficult time selling it to publishers. They didn't think people would be interested in a series about English boarding school kids, and most publishers didn't think children's books made any money. However, she didn't give up. In 1997, she sold *Harry Potter* to Bloomsbury Press for $4,000. Within three years, the series made over $480 million. Today, her fortune is greater than that of the Queen of England.

J.K. Rowling had a vision, but she didn't stop there. Instead, she put everything she had into her story—her complete focus and all of her energy. The end result? She attained success beyond her wildest imagination.

How many authors write books that never gain any attention? How many people start businesses that fail to capture the imagination of the public? It may be your conscious mind that knows the facts about a product and how it can benefit a user. It's your creative mind that determines whether you inspire trust or suspicion, belief or doubt—and whether you're the kind of person who makes your dreams happen or languishes in frustration while working at a job you don't like.

That doesn't mean you will never fail. You will. Later, I'll tell you about people who have failed many times at their chosen profession, still never taking "no" for an answer. Against the advice of many, they continued to learn from their mistakes and, in the end, succeeded beyond their wildest dreams. In many ways, it was their failures that helped propel them toward their ultimate successes.

Your creative mind will lead you toward living a happy, fulfilling life. Isn't it time you learned how to tap into the power of your creative mind and put it to work for you? Great—the first step is to take a nap.

## *Sleep and the Creative Mind*

Everyone loves a good nap. Now, it's time to start making those naps work for you. Your subconscious mind is very receptive to messages while you sleep. If regulated, those messages can actually tap into the creative mind, giving it more power when you wake. Here's how it works:

During our waking hours, the conscious mind works as a censor in our brain to continually tell us we're not good enough or smart enough to achieve what we want. Pay attention to this negative self-talk. Simple statements like, "I'm so stupid," "I'll never succeed," and "I'm not good enough," can all work to sabotage your efforts, even if you don't realize it.

When you sleep, however, the conscious mind is in neutral, and it *can't interfere*. If you send your creative mind a message while you sleep, that message is allowed to sink in. Once it's been taught to take in these messages during sleep, the creative mind can actually work to eradicate those other undesirable messages you've given yourself.

What would you like to tell your creative mind while you're sleeping? Whatever it is, the way to do so is by using creative visualizations before you go to sleep. For starters, begin with the visualizations in this book. Eventually, you will create your own messages: mind-pictures of *you* having all of the dollars you would like, finding the love you want, having the health you deserve, and the abundance of happiness you deserve.

Some people might think they've tried and failed at this already. If you think so, chances are you never really got through to your creative mind. Instead, you allowed your conscious mind to take over.

Now is the time to tap into your true self. Cast out all negative thoughts, self-doubt, and self-defeat. Optimism, self-confidence, courage and wonderful new talent will be yours. If you follow the principles outlined here, the road to prosperity is yours to take.

## Visualizing an Attitude Adjustment

If there's one thing in life over which we each have power, it's our attitude. The attitude you have is your outlook on life, and outlook can often be a self-fulfilling prophecy. When you have a positive, hopeful attitude you attract more good things to you than when you're negative and no one wants to be around you. Happiness, energy and optimism attract positive forces. Not through magic, fairy dust or supernatural measures, but simply because they are more enjoyable to be around. Think about your friends. Would you rather spend time with those who are positive, happy and enthusiastic, or those who are negative and complain about everything? See—it's not mystical; it's plain common sense.

Is it time you had an attitude adjustment? You may be surprised at how a change in the way you perceive your reality can alter what your reality is. Let me explain by telling you a story about an overstressed, working mom named Mary who had basically given up.

Mary was always tired. She lacked the energy to get anything done at home or work; thus, she was surrounded by unfinished projects. Her manager didn't appreciate her lackluster approach to work and let her know in no uncertain terms that things had to change or she would be out.

Exhausted, Mary dragged herself home each evening, only to face mounds of laundry, meals to prepare, children to be cared for and, of course, leftover paperwork from her job that needed to be completed before bedtime. Everything she faced left her depleted, discouraged and overwhelmed. She felt as if she were drowning and there was no life preserver in her grasp.

That's when she decided to use a technique outlined in this book: creative visualization. By learning to envision her idea of the perfect life in her creative mind, Mary unleashed the confidence and energy she needed to actually accomplish it. Today, she's a happy, successful businesswoman who is able to juggle a demanding career and a busy home. How? By unleashing her internal power through creative visualization.

It was the change in her attitude from victim to conqueror that made the difference. Once she embedded those visual messages in her creative mind, she began believing the impossible was possible, and you know what? She succeeded.

Don't get me wrong—she didn't JUST think herself into a better life. She had to take action to fulfill her potential. However, it wasn't until she believed she could handle her situation that she actually took the steps to accomplish her goals and make her life what she wanted it to be.

Now it's your turn. Your creative mind is a powerful instrument you can use to create the life you want, no matter what you think is standing in your way.

## *Are You Sabotaging Your Own Success?*

Thought is just part of the recipe for success. Eliminating roadblocks is another. Mary was able to improve her life by changing her attitude because it was creating a major roadblock. You, too, must look at ways in which you may be sabotaging your own efforts at success.

Do you expect to fail? If so, you may be delivering a mediocre performance simply because you don't think you're capable of more, and your self-esteem is being damaged. This is a phenomenon that almost everyone must fight against. What are some of the most common ways you may sabotage your own efforts? Below are four myths that many believe and, as a result, are allowed to sabotage dreams.

## Myth 1: "I don't have what it takes."

What do you not have that you need to succeed? More education? Sign up for a night class. A better wardrobe? Go to a local thrift shop and see what you can find. More opportunities? They're out there— maybe you really aren't looking. Everyone has exactly what it takes to make it in this world, if they're willing to step out of their comfort zone and try something new and possibly hard.

## Myth 2: "I'm too shy to get along with others."

If you're allowing an innate shyness to keep you from working with others, it may be a sign your subconscious is telling you that you don't like yourself, and therefore, you don't like the way you act among other people and would prefer to stay away from them.

This doesn't have to be your reality. Your creative mind can be persuaded to change its signals. This will allow you to *like* yourself, *like* other people and enjoy sharing their good times.

## Myth 3: "My memory is bad."

Your subconscious retains an impression of everything you've heard, seen, read, felt or tasted since the day of your birth—and perhaps even an impression of everything you've thought. When you "forget," you really mean you can't access images from your subconscious mind into your conscious. The memory is there; you're just not able to retrieve it. Your conscious mind is blocked. Hours or days later it may suddenly open and you experience a rush of images as your brain accesses what you thought you had forgotten.

There are strategies to open this mind-block and improve your mental clarity. You have a perfectly good memory. Now it's time to wake it up!

## Myth 4: "I can't concentrate."

If you have trouble focusing on a single task, or if you space out frequently, it could be you've allowed your creative mind a little too much free reign. While the creative mind is a source of inspiration, ideas and energy, if you don't control it, the next fun thing can easily distract you.

As you learn to tap into your creative mind more and more, you'll begin to see why your thoughts are so powerful and how each of your actions begins with one.

This will allow you to decide to which thoughts to give power and to which to deny it to help limit many of your distractions.

To do so, direct your subconscious mind to concentrate on the concepts you want to give the most power. Simply instruct your subconscious before your next slumber (see page 38). Then, your subconscious will instruct your conscious mind to keep those concepts always in view. When this shift occurs, you'll find you have little trouble concentrating. Instead, your focus will be effortless, eliminating a lot of worry and keeping your vital energies working together to attain your goals.

## Creating a Brand New You

Take stock of the person you are right now. Are you easily flustered? Do you take control of situations or let others lead the way? Do you believe you have the power to succeed? If not, it's time to change who you are. Begin by breaking the bonds of your internal messages by taking charge of your subconscious mind.

Stop procrastinating and start getting things done. Become the cheerful, energetic, focused and poised person you know you can be—the one you sometimes imagine yourself being. Stop letting others swoop in and handle crises. It's time you take the lead with control and adopt a can-do attitude. It may seem scary, but remember—this is going to make you a better person.

When you deal directly with problems and decisions, you begin creating a new you; one who is poised and in control. Things that fluster other people will no longer agitate you.

The key to making this strategy work is simulating the *feeling* of pleasure you will experience when accomplishing the goal. Merely thinking the thoughts is not going to do the trick. You need to experience the visualization with all of your senses. Make it come alive. *Feel* the sheer pleasure and gratitude you'll experience at the completion of your goal. This is the first step to opening your mind for the possibilities that are yours for the taking. Nothing is impossible if you believe you can do it.

## *What It Means to Prosper*

You were drawn to this book because you wanted to change your life—and change your life you will. Before you begin creating your new reality, you may want to consider asking yourself what you really want. Is it money? A big house? The ability to travel? To have people turn to you for advice? Prospering means different things to different people.

For some people, becoming prosperous means being able to buy anything they want whenever they want. For others, it means being able to enjoy more time with friends and loved ones. Still others see it as living a moderate lifestyle but never having to worry how to pay the bills. To these people, having the biggest and best isn't what drives them; security is.

Write down what being prosperous means to you. Be honest with yourself. You may visualize prosperity as an unlimited supply of money, a successful relationship, true love, perfect health, a successful business or something completely different. There is no right or wrong answer. This exercise is meant to help you get a clear picture of what you're after so you can visualize your idea while completing this book and work on building it as you learn the strategies for success.

You might worry that asking for material wealth and personal fulfillment is overdoing it. It isn't. The truth is you can't really have one without the other. I learned this lesson while visiting an old friend a few years ago.

I drove up to a cozy bungalow, unsure whether it belonged to my friend. You see, he was always talking about all he'd achieved in life, so I was expecting a much bigger house. Instead, I pulled up to a small, tastefully decorated home. It contained beautiful woodwork, modern conveniences and gorgeous furnishings. It also featured the most fantastic garden area I'd ever seen.

That night as we caught up after dinner, my friend explained that he had a good job that he loved. It didn't pay much by many people's standards, but he was able to do work he believed in. His house was small, but he and his family had everything they needed, and he'd managed to pay off the mortgage many years earlier.

"I consider us to be the most prosperous family in town," he said with great pride. "We have no financial worries, no stress and we are perfectly happy."

I went to bed that night wondering what that kind of peace felt like. My friend may not have had a sports car like the one I drove, but he went to bed each night with no worries and woke up each day looking forward to going to work. I knew at that moment that I wanted a life like his—this was what it meant to be prosperous to him, and me.

If you haven't yet attained this level of happiness, you can think of it as the first stop on your journey. Upon reaching this destination, you can raise your sights once more and continue climbing to higher and higher realms. Be satisfied to reach for one goal at a time and enjoy each one as you achieve it. There's no reason to wait until you've "made it" to begin enjoying your life.

Many people possess very little desire for material goods, yet they consider themselves to be happy and abundant. This goes to show that the definition of success and prosperity is a personal matter.

At this point, I ask you an important question: "What do you really want?" For most of us, the answer is to be happy. No matter what your definition of happiness is, that's the real reason for wanting success in life. We can't lose sight of that. You may think your goal is to be wealthy when, in reality, you seek the soul-satisfying happiness that comes from having a fulfilling life.

Figure out what you really want and what prosperity means to you, and you'll more easily figure out how to get it.

## *What Would You Do if You Were Rich?*

What would you do if you were rich? It's important to ask yourself this question, because having a clear-cut vision of what you want and what you would do if you got it is essential to following the plan outlined in this book.

For many, the answer to this simple question is, "I'd quit my job, buy a new home and car, and then do nothing." That may sound good right now, but is it what you really want to do for the rest of your life? Likely it is not.

Another person may answer the same question by stating their intent to buy the business they work for and become "the boss." Odds are this person has little real interest in running the business and even fewer skills to do so. They just feel bossed around too much and want to be the one in charge for awhile.

I once asked an accountant what she would do with great wealth. I liked her answer.

"I have so many friends and relatives who aren't enjoying the best things in life. I'd like to take them, one at a time, and do things to make them happy. I might take one to a fine store and outfit her from head to toe with stylish clothes. Another I'd take on an all-expense-paid trip. Still another has a good head for business, and I'd like to help her develop a small company of her own."

The things this accountant said she'd do for others made a long and unselfish list. There was an expression of great sincerity on her face as she described what she would do with her wealth. She proved she knew the truth of the statement that happiness comes from giving happiness.

A boy in his late teens was asked the same magic question: "What would you do if you had unlimited prosperity?"

"Wow, I don't know. I think, first of all, I'd get Dad the big screen TV he's always wanted. I'd get Mom a new computer. And for me, I'd go to an Ivy League college and study engineering."

Doesn't a statement like that make you wish you could give this young person prosperity right now so he could put it to work in such a wonderful way? Now, ask yourself, "What would I do if I suddenly won the lottery?" Your answer may surprise you.

## Gaining Prosperity

These are vital questions to explore because, believe it or not, you *can* gain prosperity and abundance in any form you wish, whether that's material goods, money, mental and spiritual blessings, personal power, leadership or friendships. Now is the time to decide the kind of prosperity you're after so you can keep this vision in mind as you draft your plan to achieve it.

If you're like most of us, it's a struggle just to get through the week. Maybe you live paycheck to paycheck, always worried that the next big emergency is going to send you over a financial cliff. For you, simply having a small nest egg in the bank may be the kind of prosperity you crave.

Wealth isn't solely determined by how much money you have in your bank account. It's determined by your state of mind. Napoleon Hill, author of *Think and Grow Rich*, said, "Anything the mind can conceive and believe, the mind can achieve."

Louise Hay, who's done groundbreaking work in healing the body through transformative thought, said, "Every thought we think is creating our future."

Don't just read these statements; believe them. Your mind might conceive the *wish:* "I'd like to be a power among people. I'd like to have money—lots of it." However, if your mind truly believed that you can have all the power and money you want, then watch out—it's yours for the taking! *Wanting* it is one thing. *Believing* you can have it is the only way to get it.

Milton Hershey was born in 1857 to a family of farmers who had limited resources. Though he had little formal education, he had dreams of owning a business. He opened his own candy shop with $150 he borrowed from his aunt. After several failed business attempts, he developed the Hershey Chocolate Company. At the time of his death in 1945, he was worth $60 million. In today's dollars, that would equal roughly $1.2 billion according to measuringworth.com. No one else believed he had what it took to succeed, but he believed in himself. It was that belief that gave him the power to succeed and make millions in the process.

## Getting Rich While You Sleep

It's interesting to note that retraining your mind to believe in your own success doesn't just happen during the day. Much of the hardest work is done at night while you're sleeping.

As I pointed out earlier, we have two minds: the conscious mind and unconscious (or subconscious) mind. The conscious mind takes care of all of our thinking, scheming and planning, while the unconscious mind looks after all of the involuntary operations in the body: breathing, circulation of blood, restoration of worn tissue, etc. In addition to this, it has reasoning powers independent of the conscious mind. While the conscious mind works on one thought, the subconscious mind can devote itself to something totally different.

How do you wake up in the morning? Do you drag yourself out of bed with thoughts like, "Well, another day at the grind. Gosh, I wish I could sleep another hour or two!"? Or, do you start your day with vibrant excitement, thinking, "I feel wonderful and energetic! I'm going to accomplish a lot today."?

Why is there such great variation in how people begin their days? The way you think when you get up is due in large part to the thought pattern established in the subconscious prior to sleeping. Allowed to fester overnight, your attitude in the morning depends a great deal on the thoughts that plague your mind as you drift off to sleep.

If you go to bed with thoughts such as, "Today was pretty tough. Tomorrow's going to be a bear, and I'm not looking forward to it at all," you're apt to be restless all night while your subconscious mind mulls over the negative thoughts you gave it earlier. Is it any wonder you wake up dreading the new day?

Suppose you go to bed building on thoughts such as, "I'm going to get up and take on the world tomorrow! Today was a fairly good day, but nothing compared to what I'll make tomorrow. I'm going to turn in, have a good night's sleep and wake up early, raring to go." Isn't it easy to understand how such an established thought pattern will bounce you out of bed with enthusiasm?

# Two: The Power of Sleep

If your subconscious mind works best during rest, then it makes sense that getting a good night's sleep is imperative to your overall success. Sounds simple enough, right? Wrong! According to recent sleep studies, people suffer from insomnia more now than ever before. Here are just a few startling statistics:

- People today get 20 percent less sleep than they did 100 years ago.

- More than 30 percent of the population suffers from insomnia.

- One in three people suffer from some form of insomnia during their lifetime.

- More than half of Americans lose sleep due to stress and/or anxiety.

- Between 40 and 60 percent of people over the age of 60 suffer from insomnia.

- Women are up to twice as likely to suffer from insomnia than men.

- Approximately 10 million people in the U.S. use prescription sleep aids.

## *Why You're Struggling to Sleep*

There are many things that can keep someone from getting the rest and relaxation they need at the end of each day. Below are some of the most common culprits that keep people from enjoying a restful night's sleep.

### Worry

Considered the number-one enemy of sleep, worry can keep us awake long into the night if we allow it. What are some of the things we worry about when we should be sleeping? Finances, health, relationships, wars, jobs and the economy are all things that can disrupt our sleep. So, what can you do about it? First and foremost, be logical.

The simple fact is that worrying doesn't change anything. You may think worry is a form of preparation, but instead it's robbing you of the energy you need to actually deal with adverse situations as they arise. Besides, the things people worry the most about seldom become reality, so we waste a lot of time stressing over things that are never going to happen.

Instead of filling your subconscious mind with worrisome problems, try something completely different. Tonight when you climb into bed, tell yourself this: *While I am asleep, I am going to let my subconscious mind find solutions to all of my problems. Tomorrow it will guide me toward the right course of action.*

When you worry, you hold negative mental pictures hostage in your brain. A better solution is to visualize the ideal condition you're seeking (instead of the problematic one), and allow your subconscious mind to find a way to make the problem go away.

## Job Stress

Too many people take their work home and to bed. They allow their minds to replay an endless loop of what they should have done or said throughout the day. Reliving your workday only adds to your stress and robs you of sleep.

Avoid another sleepless night by taking a few minutes each evening before bed to review the day's events. If there is something nagging at you, give your subconscious mind permission to seek a solution while you rest. This will allow your subconscious to work for you while you sleep, instead of creating a hostile environment that keeps you from getting the rest you need.

## Guilt

Guilt can eat away at our confidence. It's our subconscious telling us we've done something wrong or haven't done all we could or should. Don't allow guilt from yesterday's troubles consume your internal thought today. Give yourself a break. Learn from your mistakes and move onto a better life and better sleep.

## Resentment

Resentment is a poison that destroys your mind and body. It can keep you from moving forward in your life and awake at night. No matter what wrongs have been done to you, don't allow the perpetrator to harm you a second time by holding onto any feelings of resentment. Remember, hatred rarely hurts the one being hated. Only the hater is hurt by these negative feelings. While it doesn't feel good to be disliked, you must force yourself not to dwell on those feelings and instead move forward positively into new relationships where you will be valued as you deserve.

## The Future

Do you use the quiet of the night to plan your future? This may sound like a good idea until you realize that the fatigue you feel from those sleepless nights can hold you back, keeping you from actually achieving your goals.

Instead of staying up half the night planning your future, try letting your subconscious mind use its power to formulate an internal plan. Give your subconscious a task to do while you sleep, such as: *While I'm asleep I want you, my subconscious mind, to help me figure out how to solve the current issues with my employees.* (Try to be as specific as possible; vague instructions aren't as helpful.)

## Fear of Death

Most people fear the unknown, and there's no greater unknown than death. If your health isn't good, those fears may be exacerbated. Even if you're completely healthy, you could allow your fear of dying in a car crash or other accident to rob you of precious sleep. Instead, try concentrating on happier things before bedtime. Live life as if you know for certain you will live well into your 90s and stop the fear of an uncertain future from robbing you of your peace.

Problems and fears have a tendency to be magnified at night. Lying in a dark room with no noise to distract you, all of your focus is on yourself, and for some people that can mean a magnification of the things keeping them awake: worry, fear, anxiety, and even planning for tomorrow.

Don't set yourself up for a sleepless night by dreading going to bed or even telling yourself you won't be able to sleep. If you tell your subconscious mind that you won't be able to fall asleep, then it will not let you. Instead, look forward to falling off to a peaceful sleep and your subconscious will allow your body to relax and drift off in no time.

## *My Secret Sleep Technique*

Have you ever noticed that in a dark room, with your eyes closed, the field within your vision is not entirely black? Usually it's gray, somewhat the color of a dusty blackboard.

If you relax fully and fix your attention on that gray-black field, you'll discover many changes taking place. Sometimes you'll notice whirling masses of changing color. Other times you may notice geometric designs: squares, circles, triangles, etc. These designs will appear in pale white outline against the dark background.

After you've experimented with this mental screen for several nights, you'll be able to see faces and people in their entirety. This little exercise will help you get your mind off whatever has been responsible for your sleeplessness. However, it isn't the whole formula for putting yourself to sleep.

When you wish to drop off to sleep, whether immediately upon retiring or after awakening during the night, follow these simple steps:

- Make certain you're fully relaxed and comfortable. See that your pajamas are not binding in any place and the sheets are smooth.

- Give your subconscious mind the proper instruction. (In the next module you'll learn about the intelligence of the subconscious mind and how it takes instructions from the conscious mind and carries them out whether they're for your good or not.)

When putting myself to sleep, I talk to my subconscious mind as though it were a visible being. Below is approximately what I say, why I say it, and how the message works.

*I'm about to drop off into restful sleep. As I do, I'm turning all of my concerns over to you. While I'm asleep, I'll receive information to guide me in the handling of my life so it's conducted in a manner best for me. I'm now on the platform of the station waiting for the sleepy-train to carry me to the land of happy dreams. While I wait, I'll amuse myself by watching—and interpreting—the many pictures that project themselves before my mind's eye. I'll awaken in the morning refreshed and eager to begin another day.*

As you learn more about the subconscious mind, you'll find it's the seat of intelligence. With its independent reasoning powers, it can work on your problems while your conscious mind is otherwise busy.

To know that while you're enjoying restful sleep, the great intelligence of your subconscious mind is finding a happy solution to your problems is, in itself, a soothing thought.

It may seem childlike to talk about the station platform and the sleepy-train, but so what? We're all just grown-up kids. What's the harm of occasionally living in the land of make-believe? There's no better time to do so than when you want to give yourself over to a safe, comfortable, restful sleep.

The human mind can't think of two things at once. The moment you start on this routine, you'll feel comfortable and all the thoughts that might otherwise haunt you will fade completely away.

Most nights I fall asleep before even completing the mental instruction. This will happen to you after you've learned from experience that this system works.

Even if you don't go to sleep immediately, don't worry. Just continue to watch the colors and pictures moving before you. It won't take long before you drift off to sleep.

## *The Importance of Pre-Sleep Routine*

Since you're learning that the subconscious mind does its best work while the conscious mind is sleeping, it makes sense to form the habit of going to sleep promptly and resting peacefully throughout the night. This section shows you how easy it is to form this habit.

Sleeplessness can sometimes be corrected by forming good bedtime habits. As with any other difficulty you may experience, please consult your physician to rule out any physical causes of sleeplessness. If there are none, try improving your physical environment before sleep.

- An hour before bedtime, turn off all television, computers and other electronic devices connected to the Internet. Though these things are fun and entertaining, they also stimulate your senses.

- Do something peaceful before bedtime, such as reading a book or meditating. This will get you in the right frame of mind for sleep.

- Don't take part in any strenuous physical exercise just before bedtime.

- Don't eat a heavy meal within four hours of bedtime.

- Avoid caffeine during the six hours before bedtime.

- Drink something soothing like chamomile tea.

- Try to have a serene bedroom. Give it a simple, peaceful design. Avoid clutter and having a television in your room.

- Have a dark bedroom. Use shades that keep out any glare from streetlights.

- Make sure your bedroom is a comfortable temperature for sleep.

- If you hear a strange sound, do be cautious, but try not to let your imagination run away with you. Chances are it's the house creaking.

- Try to ignore any ambient noise. Use earplugs if necessary. Becoming annoyed with noise will keep you up as much as the noise itself.

## Designing Your Life

Once you've mastered the art of getting a good night's sleep, it will be time to learn how to tap into the power of your subconscious mind and use it to help you design your perfect life and achieve your greatest success.

# Three: Tapping into Your Real Intelligence

We all wish a magic genie would appear to grant us three wishes—more, if we could figure out that age-old dilemma. Think about it—wouldn't you like to drift off to sleep and awaken with all of your problems solved? You may not realize it right now, but you don't actually need a genie to have this feeling. You already hold the power to make all of your dreams come true.

If you're in debt, you have a power within you to free yourself from financial obligations. If you want to move, it's well within your power to manifest the perfect home. Your personal prosperity is completely dependent on the amount of personal power you exert.

It's just like your automobile: the more pressure you apply to the accelerator, the faster you'll go.

Whether your idea of prosperity is to have a million dollars or a billion dollars, you have the power to bring it about. If your eyes just rolled because you doubt this statement, ask yourself these questions:

"How did all the millionaires out there acquire their money? Did some mystical good fortune hand it to them? Did they all inherit it?"

While it's true some millionaires inherited their money and others may have won it, the majority of the wealthy are successful people who've been using their inner power, whether they know it or not. They possess nothing more than you except, perhaps, the awareness they can accomplish things of great magnitude. Before you use education or experience as the major difference underscoring why you can't do something they can, let's discuss the first female African-American millionaire, Madame C.J. Walker.

Walker was the daughter of former slaves. Orphaned at the age of seven, she founded a beauty business in the early 20th century after having worked as a laundress for 17 years. She eventually employed over 3,000 people. She was able to access her reservoir of personal power to overcome obstacles and attain great heights.

When talking about her success, she said, "I had to make my own living and my own opportunity! But I made it! Don't sit down and wait for the opportunities to come. Get up and make them!"

Education is a wonderful thing. It can open doors to opportunities you never imagined, and it's a good idea to get as much education as possible. However, education is not everything, and it certainly doesn't guarantee success. There are plenty of unemployed graduates ready to attest to that these days.

Richard Branson, founder and chairman of the Virgin Group that consists of more than 400 companies including Virgin Atlantic Airways and Virgin Records, dropped out of school at sixteen. His strength was his ability to connect with others, and he knew conventional schooling wasn't going to help him achieve his goals.

"My interest in life comes from setting myself huge, apparently unachievable challenges and trying to rise above them… from the perspective of wanting to live life to the fullest, I felt that I had to attempt it."

Branson used the forces of his creative mind to achieve success. He's now worth an estimated $4.2 billion and is the fourth wealthiest person in the United Kingdom.

Also, I once heard about a businesswoman in New York who was on the verge of bankruptcy. Through a series of adverse conditions, she'd reached a point where her liabilities exceeded her assets by nearly

$500,000. Creditors threatened to sue her; two of them actually started litigation. Things looked so bleak it seemed inevitable she would have to close her business. She was so discouraged that she dreaded going to her office each morning because she knew she'd have to face relentless, threatening calls from creditors.

One day while reading her newspaper on the train, she saw the story of a man who had taken over a nearly bankrupt business and turned it into an outstanding success. This story inspired her. "If that man could turn a near-bankrupt business into a success, why can't I take my own near-bankrupt business and do the same?"

Without realizing it, reading the article had sparked her creative mind into action. She began thinking in terms of CAN and WILL. The next morning she hurried into the city, and the moment she entered her office door,

*Movie*

she asked her bookkeeper to give her a full list of all her creditors.

One by one she phoned these people. "Give me just a bit more time and you'll be paid in full—with interest," she said with newfound enthusiasm.

"Did you land a big contract?" one of the largest creditors asked.

"No, but I've gained something far more important," she said. "I'm inspired to make this business work, and I have new ideas I can use to accomplish just that."

The business owner's enthusiasm and inspiration allowed her to create new ideas with real merit. Her creditors believed in her proposed solutions and as a result, she drew a favorable response from each of the companies that had formerly threatened to sue her. With that settled and her mind at peace, she concentrated her efforts on finding new business. With her newly found spirit, she had no difficulty securing many worthwhile contracts. It wasn't long before her company started showing a profit.

In this case, nothing unusual happened. Business conditions were the same. The only change was in the mind of the woman who had formerly felt her business was rapidly declining.

## Using Your Subconscious to Boost Your Conscious

Your subconscious mind holds most of your power and intelligence. Most people think the conscious mind, with its ability to think, scheme, plan and reason, is naturally the mastermind behind who they are. However, as you're about to learn, the subconscious mind is the real seat of intelligence and power. No one ever has had or will have as much intelligence on the conscious level as all of us have subconsciously.

It doesn't matter whether you think positively or negatively, your thoughts and actions are continually guided by your subconscious. It's the driving force of who you are and what you will become. Therefore, it's crucial to develop the successful consciousness of the subconscious mind.

This, of course, isn't always easy. Before it can be accomplished, you must have a better understanding of the relationship between the subconscious mind and the conscious mind.

Here's a simple metaphor to illustrate how the two work together:

Most large corporations have a chief executive officer (CEO) and a chief operating officer (COO) or general manager. There may be others in high positions, but for simplicity's sake, we will only refer to the CEO and COO.

Now, let's look at the inner workings of a software company. Typically, the CEO handles the strategic planning while the COO executes those plans.

When new software is in development, the CEO will make the decision about the overall functionality of the software. These specifications are given to the COO. Designers and programmers are instructed to come up with the details, a beta version is made, testing is conducted, and improvements are implemented until the new program is ready for release, exemplifying all of the functionality originally planned by the CEO.

This relationship works a lot like the relationship between the conscious and the subconscious. The conscious mind is the CEO; the subconscious mind is the COO. The conscious mind does the thinking, planning, and evaluating while the subconscious mind carries out the orders.

Now, let's look at an average individual. He goes to work every day and does a decent job. He makes just enough money to get by. He's not rich, but he's not poor. What he is, is average. This worker never really expects more out of himself or his life. Then, a powerful message starts taking over his consciousness. He begins to think of himself as a real SUCCESS. What happens?

His COO—his subconscious mind—accepts the thought, "I AM a success," as an instruction. It's a new model ordered by the CEO—the conscious mind.

Just as the COO at the software company gives instructions to his many department heads, so too does your COO—the subconscious mind—begin sending messages to its assistants throughout your body.

Your COO knows that to be a success, you must look like one. It will make you more alert, put a spring in your step, a look of determination in your eye, and an expression in your voice that rings of success.

Most importantly, your COO will direct your thinking so you'll be guided to do the things that will make you successful.

Several years ago, a single mother came to me hoping I could help her find a job. She was in quite a predicament. Her rent was overdue, her telephone had been disconnected and the power company was about to shut off her electricity. She was afraid she wouldn't be able to provide for her child.

I asked her to repeat, "I AM a success," frequently for the subsequent 24 hours, particularly before bedtime. This seemed a little silly to her, but I made her promise to do it.

The next morning she awoke and had such an urge to go out and prove she was a success that she sprang out of bed, eager to get to work. Leaving her house, instead of dragging along with the feeling it would be another hopeless day, she marched with her chin up and with a mental attitude telling her she was facing a world of opportunities, and she could literally select the one of her choice.

Passing a department store, this revitalized woman saw a small sign in one of the windows that read, "Display Designer Wanted." She stared at the sign for a moment, and then walked into the store with determination. In the personnel department she faced the human resources person whose responsibility was hiring employees.

LORI

"I've had no experience in display design, but I love interior design, and I believe I would do an excellent job in the position advertised in your window." The courageous and confident manner in which this applicant approached the human resources manager made an immediate good impression. The hiring manager asked only a few questions.

"I'd like to give you a chance to show what you can do. Can you start tomorrow morning?" the person behind the desk asked.

This was several years ago. The woman is now manager of her department and makes a good salary. Her creative talents have been put to good use. She has purchased a comfortable home, drives a new car and is a very good provider for her child.

The average person feels the road to success is long and arduous. Our story proves just the opposite. This one woman found an entirely new life in just 24 hours. How? By changing her thought process.

After the pattern of success was implanted in her subconscious mind, she became successful.

I hope this is a revelation to you. You no longer have to wish for a better life. The life you want is already within your grasp. All you have to do is tap into the power of your subconscious mind. This strategy doesn't just work to attain business success and wealth. It can also be used to improve your relationships or find lasting love.

A friend of mine in college was perpetually lonely. He always bemoaned the fact he was not attractive to the opposite sex and he was destined to a life of loneliness. After changing his thought process by telling himself, "I'm attractive to women. I'll meet the woman I can make happy and who, in turn, will make me happy," he met a great gal and got married. That was 10 years ago and they're still happily together.

Stories of this kind might lead you to believe that I'm exaggerating, but I'm not. This is merely evidence of what the subconscious mind can do for you when you demand it do so. Initially, my bachelor friend wasn't friendly enough. He was selfish to the extent of not thinking of anyone but himself. By giving himself new instructions and retraining his subconscious, his entire demeanor changed, and he was instantly a new man. My single mother friend was insecure about her own power and talents; she gave herself new instructions and rose to the opportunities that presented themselves to her.

You can do the same as these two and become a success at whatever it is you're after, but you must be serious about it. Don't think, "Hey, that sounds good, I'll have to try that sometime." Instead, do it today. You'll never know the potency of your subconscious mind until you actually use it.

But, be careful. Do not approach your subconscious mind negatively. Be definite about your goals and actions. Remember, the instructions you give your subconscious mind are the instructions your entire being will follow—make them count.

Think of something good you'd like to have happen. As an example, suppose you have to make an important decision tomorrow. At the moment you're in a quandary; you don't know which course to take. Instead of letting indecision rule, begin thinking something powerful and positive, such as:

*Regarding the decision I must make, I'll be guided to take the steps that are best for all parties concerned.*

Repeat this several times throughout the day and before going to bed. Know that by the time you have to reach your decision, the plan to follow will be clear to you. You'll be amazed to find how logical your thinking is, and you'll instinctively know your opinion is sound.

Don't stop there. Give your subconscious mind another task. You can't overdo it. It's always ready to serve you; all it needs is instructions. Your subconscious mind is never idle. It's always working, so why not let it work for you by guiding its decisions and the path you will follow?

## You Are What You Think

When someone says, "You're a very sweet person," what does it mean? Does it mean the "sweet" person's physical being is sugary? Does it mean the person's features portray sweetness? Is it the smile and expression that prompt the statement that the person is sweet? The answer to all of these questions is no.

Not many people realize it, but it is the mind that reflects sweetness or its opposite. A *sweet* individual is one whose mind causes him or her to be generous, understanding, sympathetic, friendly and helpful.

When we think of someone as having a magnetic personality, it's natural to associate that personality with the visible, physical being. However, this is not correct. There are beautiful people with personalities so disagreeable they're actually repulsive. There are people with plain features whose personalities are so magnetic they appear to be attractive and beautiful.

What's the difference between these people? It's a matter of mind. The latter think in terms of giving, but the former think only in terms of receiving.

Imagine two men very much alike from a physical standpoint. One man is a good businessman. He makes money and saves money. The other one just gets by. He earns a small income and spends every cent of it.

What's the difference between these two people? It's a matter of mind. One man thinks in terms of good business and sound investments. The other thinks in terms of earning solely for the pleasure of spending.

There is no important physical difference between success and failure. Again, it's a matter of controlling your thinking. One person sees herself as a failure; the other *knows* she is a success. Looks have nothing to do with it in either case.

As we make these comparisons, we have to conclude that the most important part of a human being is the mind. The mind is what we have to work with to create our destinies.

You are what you visualize yourself to be. That doesn't mean you are "you" because you're tall or short, dark or light, overweight or underweight. It means that the "you" people like or dislike is a reflection of your mind.

You don't have to be unhappy. You don't always have to complain. You *can* be successful. In other words, within the realm of your great mind is the power and intelligence to guide your life in any direction you choose.

The most successful corporations are guided by a single person. Of course, that person has many associates who collaborate on projects, but there must be a mastermind to guide the company.

When Steve Jobs and Steve Wozniak introduced the first Apple computer in 1976, they changed the world. While companies like IBM thought people would never have personal computers in their homes, Jobs and Wozniak believed differently. Over the years, Apple Computers revolutionized our lives in so many ways. Though the many products created by Apple were the product of collaboration, Jobs was the visionary who headed this groundbreaking company. Their revolutionary (and often emulated) advertising slogan was, "Think Different."

Steve Jobs once said, "Your work is going to fill a large part of your life, and the only way to be truly satisfied is to do what you believe is great work. And the only way to do great work is to love what you do. If you haven't found it yet, keep looking. Don't settle. As with all matters of the heart, you'll know when you find it."

You have within your mental self a gigantic reservoir of power, most of which is unused. Just as the pilot drives a plane, the captain steers a ship, the engineer speeds the train, you, your conscious mind, can steer your subconscious mind so it'll guide you in any direction you select, to achieve anything you desire. Health, wealth and happiness are easily within your grasp.

## Who Are You? Ask Your Mind

One of the things I am most grateful for is my curious mind. I must have been born under the sign of a question mark. The adverbs *how, why, when* and *where* are the most overworked words in my vocabulary.

I first learned to drive a car with a manual shift. I wasn't satisfied with being told how I should move the shift to change gears. So, I opened the lid of the gearbox to see what happened when I moved the lever.

I've always been like that. "Why does it work?" and "How does it work?" are questions I always ask.

Several years ago, while having dinner with a friend, we began discussing the mysteries of humankind. We talked about the power of the mind and how it directed every cell in the body. We considered that taking away the mind would leave a decaying mass of flesh and bones. It was then that a great truth dawned on me. Up to that time, I had looked at the human being as a body with a mind. But that isn't the case. *A person is a mind with a body.*

Sure, your body is important. You wouldn't live long without your physical being; but you also cannot function without the commands from your mind.

## *Are You Driven by Habit?*

A paper published by a Duke University researcher, in 2006, found that more than 40 percent of the actions we perform each day are guided by habit rather than decision-making. That's disturbing because it means we are letting old scripts rule our lives.

When you wake up in the morning, do you move in a conscious or automatic manner? The odds are good your actions are automatic. You could finish showering and dressing even if you remained asleep. Your mind isn't telling your body what to do; it already knows the drill. Your body already knows how to wash, dress, brush your teeth and eat.

The same is true when you climb behind the wheel of your car and head to work. You probably don't give a thought to the route you'll take. The car seems to go automatically. You don't think about the workings of the steering wheel, brakes, accelerator and turn signal. It all happens automatically. It's a habit.

It takes us more time to learn something new because we have to *think as we act*. When the subconscious mind takes over, we become faster and far more accurate in what we're doing. In other words, we become proficient after the act becomes a habit.

How do we apply this to our daily lives? Simple. If you're not happy with your life as it is, all you have to do is begin acting *as if* you have the life you already want. How you ask? By forming habits consistent with the life you want to live.

Habits aren't formed overnight and while they can become strongly ingrained within us, they *can* be broken, if we set out intentionally to do so.

If you're out of shape, a fitness trainer can show you how to exercise to improve your flexibility, muscle tone and strength. However, merely showing you how isn't enough to affect change within your body. You must establish a routine, and then follow it consistently for a period of time before there is a noticeable change in your body.

If you're not successful, not happy, always hurting and complaining, it's because you're being guided by the habits that make these conditions a reality. Maybe you think you're a failure, and you don't deserve success. This is more common than you think. Conditioning in early life can cause individuals to believe they are not worthy of success and happiness.

A friend of mine, who is now very successful, told me a story that illustrates my point.

"I overheard my friends talking about me, and it changed my entire life. I'd always been kind of a slacker, just getting by, but I often talked about the big things I was *going* to do. One day a friend of mine said, 'Ryan is a nice enough guy, but he's a daydreamer. He always says he's going to do something, but never actually does it.' I decided then and there I was going to turn my dreams into reality."

Ryan changed his thought pattern. The "slacker/daydreamer" thought nagged at him until he created a new picture of himself. He began seeing himself as a *doer* instead of a *talker*. In a short amount of time, his new mental picture was complete, and he became an outstanding success.

## Breaking the Habit of Negativity

It's difficult to see negativity within ourselves. When questioned, we'd probably say we aren't negative at all. Yet those around us may see a very different attitude.

Want to know if you're negative without even realizing it? Here's a simple test that will tell you, in no uncertain terms, whether your mind leans toward the negative or positive.

Below are 25 ordinary words. Read each word slowly and write down the first mental image that pops into your mind.

1. love

2. mountain

3. money

4. automobile

5. food

6. sex

7. dark

8. book

9. rest

10. law

11. water

12. letter

13. garden

14. maid

15. boss

16. home

17. guests

18. health

19. animal

20. father

21. clothing

22. music

23. children

24. write

25. tests

Compare the images you wrote for each word with the negative and positive notes below. Circle all of the words for which your image matched the negative point instead of the positive one.

## Positive and Negative Notes

*Love.* The association flashing in the mind of a negative person might be: No one loves me. On the other hand, a mental picture of a loved one might appear in the mind of the positive thinker.

*Mountain.* The negative person could easily picture dangerous rocks on which his clothing could become torn, or he could be hurt falling off a high cliff.

Mountains add beauty to the environment in the mind of the positive thinker.

*Money.* Negative: debts, lack of it, etc. Positive: comfort, security, generosity.

*Automobile.* Negative: lack of one, or condition of present car. Positive: enjoyable trips, fun for the family.

*Food.* Negative: poor meals, indigestion, obesity. Positive: pleasant repast with relatives and friends, normal weight.

*Sex.* Negative: resentment if not happy with mate, or if unpopular with opposite sex. Positive: happiness, fulfillment, blissful relationship.

*Dark.* Negative: loneliness. Positive: rest, relaxation.

*Book.* Negative: study, boredom. Positive: enlightenment, pleasant pastime.

*Rest.* Negative: works too hard; no time for rest. Positive: recuperation, recreation.

*Law.* Negative: traffic tickets. Positive: order, protection.

*Water.* Negative: drowning, rain. Positive: swimming, boating, cleanliness.

*Letter.* Negative: bad news. Positive: good news.

*Garden.* Negative: work, expense. Positive: healthful exercise, beauty.

*Maid.* Negative: can't afford one. Positive: lifts the load of housework.

*Boss.* Negative: slave driver. Positive: promotion, income.

*Home.* Negative: fighting, nagging. Positive: companionship with family.

*Guests.* Negative: extra work and expense. Positive: great times with good friends.

*Health.* Negative: awareness of aches and pains. Positive: a condition worth striving for.

*Animal.* Negative: a nuisance, expense. Positive: loyalty, devotion, companionship.

*Father.* Negative: strict, never gave any breaks. Positive: love, devotion, support.

*Clothing.* Negative: small wardrobe, cheap clothing. Positive: quality clothes, well cared for.

*Music.* Negative: noise, annoyance. Positive: peace, inspiration.

*Children.* Negative: pests, expense. Positive: fulfillment.

*Write.* Negative: inability to write causing one to dread writing. Positive: helps one to develop ideas.

*Tests.* Negative: lack of faith in one's ability to pass. Positive: gives one an opportunity to try his or her skill.

If you find more words are circled than are not, it's definitely time for a change. While many of these words may seem on the surface to be negative, each has the capacity to be positive, if you think of them that way. Being aware of your negativity is half the battle. Since a positive attitude has a direct correlation to success, chances are that if you're negative, you're not enjoying as much success as you might.

## *Becoming a Positive Person*

Yes, you can learn to become more positive! Here are a few tips to get you started:

- *Make a list of your positive qualities.* Take a difficult situation and list as many positive aspects about it as you can. Start out general and work your way toward the specifics. For example, if you are referring to money, you might say:

- Having money gives me a good sense of security. Money is useful for paying bills. I like the feeling of having extra money.

Gradually, you will work your way to saying: I feel prosperous, and I have all the money I'll ever need. This will start you on the road toward being more positive in that one area.

- *Make an appreciation list.* Make a list of all the things you are thankful for in your life. This can go from the smallest (I love the colors of the flowers in the park.) to the largest (I'm thankful for the love of my family.). The more you appreciate, the more good things will come to you. It's a law of the universe.

- *Turn your self-talk from negative to positive.* This is something I discovered for myself at a time when I was trying to make positive changes in my life. I took part in a lot of negative self-talk. I'd make a mistake and say to myself, "Oh, you're such an idiot," or "No wonder you're not successful, you're a slacker."

For a day, pay attention to all of the unkind things you say to yourself—things you wouldn't dream of saying to someone you love but don't hesitate to say to yourself. Every time you find yourself saying something negative to yourself, stop. Replace it with something positive. Soon it will become a habit.

- *Make a file of positive affirmations.* Get a set of index cards and make a list of positive affirmations, such as:
  - *I let go of the fears that drain my energy.*
  - *I'm finding my perfect love.*
  - *I'm prosperous. Money is my friend.*
  - *I have abundant energy and enjoy perfect health.*

- *My body maintains its perfect weight, easily and effortlessly.*

Take out these cards and read them often. Single out one per day to focus upon. Add to them when the inspiration arises.

## The "I Can Do It!" Plan

Utilization of the techniques above is a good way to begin retraining your mind to think and act more positively, but that's not all you can do. I have devised a very simple and effective way of re-educating your subconscious mind to make it naturally think more positively. Here's what to do:

For a full week, say, "I CAN be a success!" to yourself as often as you think of it. Say it before going to sleep, when you first wake up, and several times during the day.

This allows your mind to see your potential for success as fact. Your subconscious already knows that unless you know you are able to succeed, there's little use in trying to do so. Burn this truth into your mind, even if at first, you don't believe it. After a short period of time, you'll begin rejoicing in the thought that success can be yours.

Knowing you can be a success isn't enough, though. We all know lots of things we *can* do, but unless we actually do something about them, the positive knowledge is of little benefit. This brings us to the second phase of the formula. For another full week, you can take longer if you wish, every time you think of it, repeat to yourself: "I WILL be a success." Do this many times from early morning until you fall asleep at night.

Watch as changes begin taking place in the way you think, feel and act. As these messages become reality in your subconscious mind, you'll begin experiencing a type of pleasant uneasiness. You'll itch to begin testing your new powers. For example, if you've yearned for a business of your own, you'll suddenly have the urge to start planning for one. You'll start looking at rental properties, checking out financing options online and investigating suppliers. Whatever you need, your subconscious mind will guide you toward ways to get it.

Now that the ball is rolling on your success acquisition, don't stop. There's more work to do. For at least another week, begin telling yourself, "I AM a success." Do this frequently from early morning until bedtime.

This statement may seem to be a bit premature, but it isn't. If you have money in the bank, but none in your pocket, you know that, without effort, you can write a check and obtain money. If you have a *success consciousness* and know you CAN and WILL be a success, you have a fulfillment of your desire.

These principles work, but do not take my word for it. Give them a good try, and experience the results.

# Four:

# Getting to Know the Real You

Many people, whether they realize it, lean toward the negative in their thinking. This explains why such a large percentage of people are unhappy and, based on their own personal definitions of success, unsuccessful.

If you found, after completing the test in the last module, that you're one of those who lean toward the negative side, you might not be particularly pleased to meet the real YOU. However, that's just your fear and negativity talking. Instead of being regretful when meeting your true self, you will now understand why you're negative and unhappy. This is cause for celebration because you're now empowered to change your situation—something you can't do when you're in denial.

Once you come to grips with the person you are, you can begin changing the way you think, which will change the way you live. Think of this process like learning a magic trick. You watch the magician do the trick over and over again, each time more baffled at how he can accomplish it without anyone figuring out the illusion. Then, the magician shows you how he does the trick. The mystery is gone. What seemed impossible just a few minutes earlier is suddenly within your grasp. With a little practice, you know you can do it, too.

The same philosophy can be used to change your life. So many people trudge through life believing they can't do any better. In reality, however, all they have to do is learn how the trick is done. Here's an example of how a change in mental attitude took one person out of the doldrums and into the life she wanted.

Susan White was an average person. She made enough to get by, but was certainly not a person classified as successful. When one of her friends got married, she went to see the newlywed's new home. It was a jealousy-inducing, six-bedroom home complete with an in-ground pool, sauna, game room and home theater. Susan was struck by how much more her friend had than her. She left her visit feeling depressed and unhappy.

"Why should she have everything?" she wondered. Then it hit her, "Why am I so unhappy? Right now I have everything she has: a nice home, a great husband, good friends and lots of stuff. Sure, her stuff is more elaborate, but I was happy before I went to see her new house. Why am I unhappy now?"                    Marle

As Susan made comparisons between her situation and that of her friend, she began to understand she was not off too badly and felt a sense of peace settle over her. However, she didn't allow herself to become complacent. She began developing what I refer to as *happy discontent*. She was happy with the life she had, but not content to remain satisfied with it since she felt she could, and had the right to, have more.

Envy is a limiting trait. To envy indicates a lack of confidence in one's ability to acquire what is envied. In so doing, envy prevents the development of initiative to obtain what is being envied. Susan realized that, even without riches, she could enjoy the same blessings her friend had and this gave her a great sense of peace. She no longer envied her friend, but found she was growing mentally and could begin thinking in terms of self-improvement.

She started taking college classes on th

earned her master's degree in busir

Today she's an esteemed project manager in her field

and lives in a house just a few blocks away from her

friend. Success was hers—she just had to take it.

## *Change Your Thought Patterns, Change Your Life*

Not enjoying life like you should? It's not your circumstances standing in your way; it's your attitude. Just think about how your brain ignores all the good in your life in order to focus almost obsessively on the little things bothering you. That single hair out of place, that last five pounds, that chipped paint—whatever it is that bothers you, you must block out a ton of good to focus exclusively on the bad. That's how negativity works. You may only have one small thing to feel negative about, but that bad feeling will overtake your entire attitude—if you let it.

Don't let your negative emotions and thoughts cloud an otherwise positive life. Train yourself to be positive. Every time you find yourself holding a negative thought, chase it out with a positive one. You may not see results immediately, but they will come if you are patient.

Planting positive thoughts in your mind is like planting a seed. When you sow a seed in the ground, several days pass before anything shows above the surface. However, if you cultivate and water it, you know it will produce a plant so tall and vibrant, it cannot be ignored. When you first begin holding positive thoughts, you may not see anything happen, but with persistence, you're positive side will soon take over. This change will transform your life.

"How can I be positive when everyone around me is negative?" you may ask. The answer is simple: you have a choice. You can choose to dwell on the negative or you can choose to keep a positive attitude and enjoy its benefits.

Positivity doesn't always happen automatically, especially in the beginning of your journey. You often have to work to cultivate it—just like that plant we discussed above. It's not always easy to see the positive in a situation, especially when everyone around you seems to be stuck in negativity. This is where you must know what you want and take the lead in guarding your own attitude. Don't count on others to make you happy. Instead, be determined to walk along your own pathway. Not only will your attitude help you get what you want, but it can also help others change for the better. Here is the example of a woman I know who used a well-conceived strategy to change her negative husband into an enthusiastic, positive-thinking man.

The wife—let's call her Theresa—lived with a man named Sam who was constantly complaining and finding the worst in people. "That mind-over-matter stuff is nonsense," he constantly grumbled. Whenever Theresa voiced a more positive attitude, she was told she was "not facing reality."

Theresa could have resigned herself to a life of mediocrity, but she refused. She knew the laws of positive thinking, and she also knew how her husband was holding himself back by his own negative thoughts. So, she came up with a plan.

One evening while Sam was sitting around doing nothing in particular, Theresa busied herself by reading one of the many books on mental self-improvement. "I can't really understand this. Will you read part of this chapter and see if you can make out what the author is trying to say? You're so good at figuring out things," she said, as she handed the open book to her husband.

Softened by her flattery, he accepted the challenge. He read the chapter, not intending to agree with the author but to find loopholes whereby he could prove to his wife that all mind-over-matter theories were nonsense.

But as Sam read on and on, the material he was reading began to make sense to him; it all added up. He slowly accepted the idea that negative thoughts produce negative reactions and positive thoughts produce positive reactions.

Sam began thinking about his job. He realized he lived by the motto, "Do what's expected and no more." The next morning he left for work with a new attitude. He decided to give his job 100 percent. In his eagerness to excel, he even made a discovery: he learned a shortcut that enabled him to turn out more, and better, work. Others in the company could even use his discovery to make their efforts more efficient. Then, you know what happened? Sam put this approach into play and was promoted. Today he's the head of training and sales for a large corporation.

What turned this negative man into someone who aspired for more and succeeded? The power of positive thinking. This man changed his thought process, which changed his attitude, which helped him improve his work ethic and receive the recognition he's always wanted.

Not everyone believes the mind can produce real-life changes. Think of it like this: the person who remains miserable through failure, poor health and gloom is definitely being influenced by mind over matter. That person doesn't *wish* for these conditions, but *sees* him- or herself as being stuck with them; he or she *believes* they are doomed to possess them. That is exact result they get.

If this same person could visualize—just as strongly— health, wealth and happiness, not *wish* for them, but see him- or herself possessing them, doesn't it make sense that such positives could be achieved?

I hope this module inspires you to want more for yourself. I hope you're beginning to allow your vision for what *can* be to pierce through the fog of uncertainty and doubt, so you can get a glimpse of the new life that will be yours. I hope this because I know there's much more awaiting you, if only you believe it exists.

# Five: Attracting Success through Visualization

You see it all the time: people stuck in their situation because they can't see themselves living any other kind of life.

- The fast-food worker who doesn't even dream of becoming the manager.

- The middle-aged employee who gives up on dreams of being promoted to management because if he or she hasn't been yet, they're never will be.

- The professional who gets stuck in a certain position because they can't visualize themselves making it to the top and being the boss.

Maybe you tell yourself you're not musical or artistic or good with computers. Well, you're not now, but that isn't because you have no talent or skill. It's because you haven't tried to master these things without negativity interrupting the process. Our bodies don't dictate what we're good at; our minds do. When we tell ourselves we can't do something, then we can't. The good news is that the opposite is also true.

Several years ago I was talking with a friend's mother. During the conversation, she confessed she'd always dreamed of painting landscapes. "What's stopping you?" I asked. "Simple," was her reply. "I have absolutely no artistic talent, but I sure would like to paint just a single picture before I die."

That year for Mother's Day, my friend bought her 80-year-old mother a class with a local artist who promised every student would leave his day-long demonstration with a completed landscape. His entire philosophy was that skill was not needed. All you needed were the tools to succeed and a good attitude walking into the class. He could teach you the rest.

My friend's mother entered the class feeling a bit apprehensive. The painting on the easel at the front was beautiful. She had no grand delusion she'd be able to finish one like it by the end of the day. Then, she started talking to other students who encouraged and assured her they, too, entered their first class with the same mix of feelings and doubt and walked out in the afternoon with a beautiful painting they'd finished all by themselves. She began to feel more confident and told herself that if they could do it, so could she.

She spent the morning and afternoon creating a masterpiece one small stroke at a time. By day's end, she had a painting that looked just as good as everyone else's. It was beautiful! She had succeeded. Inspired, she went home and used the same technique to paint another picture that same evening. Today, she has dozens of paintings adorning her walls.

Did this woman suddenly, at the age of 80, develop artistic talent? No! The only thing that changed was her thinking. Once she met someone who made her believe anyone could paint a picture, she was able to do just that—and many more.

Is there something you've always wanted to do but thought you couldn't? Well, let me give you a bit of good news—once you become aware that you can do it, you'll have no trouble getting it done. Just as a pebble dropped in a lake causes ripples all the way out to the shore, your thoughts can create a ripple of confidence and ability to shoot through your mind. One new thought dropped into your mind's pool ripples into every facet of your life until you accomplish exactly what you once dreamed impossible. The key is to believe in that possibility and not allowing negativity to squelch your efforts.

## The Creation of You

Have you ever thought about why you are the way you are? Why are you kind, considerate or generous rather than short-tempered, nasty and opinionated? Most people just accept who they are and never really consider why they think or act certain ways.

Most of us develop our personalities as children. It's during these formative years that fears, phobias, inhibitions and neuroses begin molding who we are and will become. Consider the anxiety-riddled person. Very few people suddenly start exhibiting the traits of extreme anxiety as adults. Instead, trauma or information that was delivered to them as children becomes magnified in their minds, ripples through their entire adulthood, and constrains their confidence and potential.

A mother might wish to show off little Jennifer before guests. She may ask her to recite or to sing. For some reason, Jennifer hesitates; her mother, without realizing the damage she is doing, comments on how Jennifer is afraid of failure.

Such comments, in the presence of a child, create a persona that the child believes about him- or herself. As Jennifer grows up, she considers herself to be afraid of failure, wishing she could put herself out there and take risks, but admits that she can't because she fears failure. Those of us who know anything about the workings of the mind know that every time Jennifer gives voice or thought to her fear, she makes it worse. So, this woman goes through life missing much enjoyment because of a fear that may have never really existed.

Research has shown that many people who find success just beyond their grasp had the failure instinct instilled in their minds when they were children and are held back by a sense of inadequacy.

"Get away from that—you'll break it. You don't know anything about tools." Children are always told about the things they *can't* do but are seldom given credit for the things they *can* do. Fewer still are instilled with curiosity about their potential. Sadly, these children grow into adults who believe these statements as truisms. They often grow up repeating things their parents said without questioning their accuracy. Illustration after illustration can be given showing us why we are as we are. In most cases, a pattern is fixed in our minds that we are "this way" or "that way" and from then on, we reflect that condition. Consider the child who doesn't like crust on her sandwiches—and let's face it, most of us were that child. But as we grew up, we didn't continue to insist people cut our crusts off for us. Instead, we eventually tried to eat bread with a crust and, you know what? We liked it.

*You are what you visualize yourself to be.* If your parents were wise enough to implant in your mind that you had the makings of a wonderful artist, you would continue to see yourself as such and, in later years, you would reproduce in your life the picture you had of yourself.

It's encouraging to realize that no matter what influences you've had in your life, you *can* be anything you want to be.

## Transform Yourself

How long would it take to change yourself from what you are to what you'd like to be? That's a good question, and the answer is interesting and even inspiring.

Any type of transformation takes time and a certain amount of effort. Once you begin to become aware of the things you can do, your subconscious mind will start finding ways to make you better at those things.

Until you believe you can accomplish a goal, success will be fleeting. Once you accept the fact you can and will succeed, you'll begin seeing yourself play out this new role by expanding your offerings and growing in both confidence and skill.

Let's assume you've always envied people who were business owners. You never tried to get into a business of your own because you were afraid—afraid you lacked the ability to run a business and that you might fail. However, suppose you re-educated your subconscious mind to see yourself as a person who could build a successful business. What would happen? After deciding on the type of business you'd enjoy, you take the necessary steps to establish it. The success you attain would depend entirely upon the clarity of the mental pictures you have of yourself as a person who is business savvy. The stronger the impression, the greater your success will be.

I cannot overemphasize that you do not merely *wish* for the change you want. Wishing will not bring about the desired outcome. When you wish for something, it's an indication you don't expect to get it—otherwise you wouldn't wish for it, you'd prepare for it.

You have to *know* you're a good programmer, a fluent writer, a great musician—or anything else you'd like to be. See yourself as the exact kind of person you want to be, accomplishing the goals you set. Then, watch as you begin transforming into that exact person accomplishing those exact things.

No matter who you are today, you can become better tomorrow by literally changing your mind. Go to bed each night with thoughts about your future. Don't wish for a change; see the change. Burn it into your mind and experience change like you never knew possible.

## *Don't Underestimate What You Can Do*

Are you good at your job? Really good? Do you have any idea how good you really are? Probably not. If you haven't actively tested your abilities and tried to improve, you have no idea of what you're capable.

I know a salesperson named Bob who realized he'd spent his whole life underestimating himself and, when he realized that, he discovered his own philosophy and changed the way he thought of himself in order to produce better results at work.

Bob sat in a sales meeting and listened as the speaker explained that each person on the floor was twice as good as he/she thought they were. That thought intrigued Bob, and he decided to prove—or disapprove—the notion. He went over his recent sales and then reviewed his client lists and sales calls. That's when he noticed something. He wasn't getting any supersized orders, and for good reason: he wasn't contacting the clients who could give him those big orders. That's when Bob made some important decisions:

1) First, he started calling customers who were able to place big orders.

2) He hustled more, making more sales calls than he ever had.

3) He worked at strengthening his sales skills so he could increase his success rate.

Over the next few weeks, an amazing transformation took place. Bob wasn't twice as good as he thought he was—at the end of the month, he was astonished to discover his sales increased by 100 percent. Bob discovered the key to success—believing he could increase his sales and then following through with specific action steps to make that belief a reality.

Bob isn't the only one who can benefit from this business strategy. Take Nancy, a young woman who launched an Internet start-up a few years ago. Soon after the big launch she found herself discouraged that her new social networking site was not attracting many visitors. Once she realized she wasn't living up to her full potential, she challenged herself to add new features to the site. She found an untapped audience and started marketing to those people. Within months her subscriptions soared, and she was able to hire employees to expand her business. Once Nancy realized she was capable of more, she began to reap the benefits of more—much more.

Are you like Bob and Nancy, struggling to keep your head above water and working under the delusion this is all you're capable of? If so, you may want to ask yourself why. The reason may be an inability to see your true potential and worth. Stop underestimating your own abilities, and start seeing your true potential. Then, and only then, will you be able to tap into the power to expand your opportunities and increase your wealth.

## *Making Progress*

Wouldn't you love to double your income this year? That may sound impossible, especially during these difficult economic times, but it isn't. Let's assume you really are twice as good as you think you are. You should be able to increase your outcome and double your income.

"Yeah, right," you may be thinking. "Easier said than done." That's a negative response. Remember what we said about negativity earlier—if you think negatively, then negative things will happen. See yourself being twice as good as you are right now, and you will become twice as good at your job.

This is all due to cause and effect. Let me explain. A large income is not a cause, it's an effect. It's the result of ideas put into action. Ideas are the generators of success. Industries, fortunes, even empires have been built on the powerful foundation of ideas. Everything you buy is the result of an idea. None of us will doubt the value of good constructive ideas, but strangely enough, only a few people have any faith in the value of their own ideas.

"If that idea was any good, someone else would've thought of it." You hear this expression all the time, yet in many cases the abandoned idea forms the basis of an outstanding success—by someone else.

Let me give you a few examples showing the value of *simple* ideas, and then I'll show you how to make your mind a veritable fountain of ideas.

In New York, a video game packager advertised a computer graphics animator position opening. There was one young woman who wanted the job, and she decided she'd go further than writing a letter of application. The job was a great opportunity, and she knew there would be tons of applicants vying for it.

She researched the company so she knew everything about it before she attempted to apply. She also researched the most popular video games and what other features players would like to see in them.

She put the information she gathered into the form of an online presentation with a sample of her own video game animation at the end. Next, she went to the manager of the company and arranged for an interview. She showed him her presentation and told him she had ideas about increasing company sales.

The manager was so happy with her initiative, he hired her immediately. That was the start of her happy, profitable career as a video game animator.

In Chicago, a young man wanted a position with one of the more prominent advertising agencies. He also wanted to go beyond sending the usual resume and cover letter. The young man found a way of meeting one of the heads of the company he had selected. He approached this individual with this unusual statement: "Ms. Smith, I believe I can add to the value of your agency. Will you give me a desk and let me show you what I can do for one week? At the end of that time, you can decide if you'd like to have me continue." He was given the trial, he made good, he kept climbing and today he is vice president of the company. He had an idea—and he made use of it.

Another man left his stressful job in the city to open an antique store in a small farming town. The village was so small that if this man had all of the business in it, he could hardly make a living. Here was his problem: he liked the atmosphere of the small community, yet he needed to get more business to survive. He called upon his subconscious mind for an idea, and he got it.

He used some of the large antique magazines as a resource for email lists. He purchased some of the lists and began sending out emails. He also advertised in these national magazines and set up his own webpage.

Within several months he built a substantial online business that subsidized his small-town living. The actual physical customers visiting his store also increased. This man used his creative talents to increase his income and maintain his version of an ideal, prosperous life.

Every patent in the United States Patent Office is the result of an idea. Who had these ideas and developed them? Regular people, just like you and me, thought of a large percentage of these ideas.

It's often said there are so many patents that it's becoming increasingly difficult to conceive new ones. This, of course, isn't true. Each new patent issued opens up avenues for countless more patents. It's obvious to us today there is no limit to innovation. The Internet, laptops, tablets and smartphones have paved the way for millions of new patents on new programs, apps and peripherals. So, we find that instead of opportunities for invention decreasing, they're multiplying rapidly. Just watch one episode of "Shark Tank" or "Dragon's Den," a home-shopping infomercial or glance through a catalogue, and you'll see one new invention after another.

Every time anything goes wrong, any time you see an unfulfilled need, you have an opportunity for an invention.

Sara Blakely saw an opportunity for a product the public needed, and she took it. Frustrated by VPL (visible panty lines) and uncomfortable thongs, she invented footless pantyhose, called Spanx. This invention grew into a national brand and led a shapewear revolution. Obsessed with creating comfortable, slimming garments that minimize figure flaws, Blakely has created more than 150 problem-solving products.

She now sells her products online, on television shopping networks and in department stores. Many celebrities love to wear Spanx while walking the red carpet to make their figures appear smooth under form-fitting dresses. She now has a multinational, multimillion-dollar business, all because she saw a need and filled it.

Ideas are crystallized thought, or thought that has taken form. They are a foundation on which to build. Every place you look you see ideas that have become realities. Every business is built upon an idea. The clothes you wear, the house you live in, the automobile you drive all resulted from ideas.

You can struggle all your life without making much progress, when suddenly a single idea can lift you out of obscurity into the limelight of success and happiness. There's no age limit to those who may develop ideas of value. Regardless of age, you have a unique perspective you can use to your advantage.

I know that you have within your mental make-up all that's necessary to form ideas valuable to humanity, and at the same time will reap valuable rewards for you. Here are three steps on how to condition your subconscious mind to generate ideas at will—ideas to assist you in any direction you may wish to travel, ideas to help you prove, conclusively, you're at least twice as good as you think.

## Step 1. See Yourself as Creative

You've already learned that the way to create an *awareness* of any truth is by instructing your mental self. The development of ideas is no exception. To have a fertile mind capable of creating new and important ideas, you must *see* yourself as being creative. Make positive affirmations regarding your idea-producing mind, such as:

*My mind is alert and active, continually bringing into consciousness a flow of constructive ideas valuable to humanity.*

Whenever you do anything of creative nature, precede your action with the suggestion just given or make up one of your own. Notice how your ideas flow. If you are writing an email, a blog post or a book, you won't be at a loss for words if you follow this routine.

## Step 2. Cultivate Your Curiosity

Develop within your mind an *idea-consciousness*. Become *happily discontented* with things as they are. Look for ways to improve the things in your life. Whether it's your coffee maker, toothbrush or car, always ask yourself this important question: "What can I do to improve this?"

If you're employed, study the work you're doing. How can you do it better or faster? Approaching your work with such an attitude will make it far more enjoyable. The time will pass more quickly and pleasantly and, from your constructive thinking, ideas may come into being that will reward you for your greater interest and efforts.

## Understanding Happy Discontent

You can be discontent with your life as it is, but still be happy. I like to refer to this as happily discontent. Basically, it means wanting more out of your life, knowing you can have more, and going after it—but not being unhappy or putting your life on hold as you work toward it.

Newlyweds often master the art of happy discontent. Just starting out in their lives together, they've rarely achieved the kind of professional success they ultimately want. They may someday want to own a home, start a family or move to another part of the country. While they work toward these mutual goals, they still enjoy the novelty of being newly wed. At no point are they unhappy with their current circumstances; they simply know they want more for the future.

## Step 3. Start an Idea File

An idea becomes something tangible the moment you do something about it. An idea has its greatest intensity at the time of its birth. How often have you had ideas and thought to yourself, "That's a good one—I'll definitely remember it later," only to completely forget it? That's why it's so important to preserve them before they begin fading. Each time an idea comes into your consciousness, write it down. Write down everything that comes into mind related to that idea. The very act of describing the idea in writing prevents it from fading; that's why keeping a journal of your ideas is so very important. If you can, make a sketch of your idea.

Remember: the more you do in connection with the idea, the bigger it grows.

Review your ideas frequently to keep them alive in your mind. Also, should you have additional ideas pertaining to those already in your file, bring it up to date by adding the new thoughts.

A data-entry person in an insurance company was bored doing the same thing eight hours every day. He didn't think creativity played any part in his work. After becoming conscious of the fact his mind could and would create new ideas even without his prompting, he began, with open eyes, to study his work. He thought of ways to streamline processes. When he presented these ideas to his manager, she was reluctant at first but then investigated his ideas. Finally, she put them into practice. Eventually, he was promoted for his good ideas and no longer had to perform data entry. You have great ideas, too. Don't keep them a secret.

## *The Power of Focus*

Some modern-day entrepreneurs are like rock stars, Steve Jobs founded Apple Computers in his garage, Bill Gates founded Microsoft based on the DOS operating system and Oprah Winfrey started as a reporter and used her experience to create a multimedia empire.

How did they achieve such greatness? What do they have in common?

They all had a ***singular vision*** and they ***focused*** on it to the exclusion of everything else. People may have told them they were crazy to think they could succeed, but it didn't matter. They persevered. They had a dream, and they followed it relentlessly. In the 1970s, the big computer companies thought people would *never* have computers in their homes, that computers would only be in big businesses. Well, they were wrong, and the people who had the vision to see that became very successful.

## Focus on Your Bliss

These words are among the most potent ones in our language. Pessimism creates a mental structure that prevents the flow of constructive thoughts. However, following your bliss is about allowing the positivity and creativity to carry you to your next great adventure. Think of the times when you were gloomy and sad. Were you inspired to do big things? Did you conceive ideas that could add to your prosperity? Did you feel ambitious to blaze new trails? The answer to all of these questions is, of course, no.

Think of the times when you were exuberant, when every fiber of your being was shining with joy. Didn't you have the urge to go places and do things? Projects that under normal conditions might appear laborious probably seemed like nothing at all. That, you see, is bliss.

Follow your bliss. If you have problems, which we all do from time to time, be happy that the knowledge they give you allows you to learn to master obstacles. If you give in to negativity, you will allow your problems to master you instead of the other way around.

# Six:

# Your Finances—Fact or Fiction?

Humans tend to hold money, and those who have it, in high esteem. After all, it's essential if we want to get what we want. Without money, we can't have our heart's desire. Money is what drives us, yet money isn't even real. It's a mutually agreed-upon method of trade; a concept for achieving.

We strive for more money in our bank accounts so we can have what we want, but it isn't really the money we're working for. It's the end result of what that money can buy: security, food, shelter and fun.

We look at money as something real. We take a dollar bill and hold it in our hands and feel we have something substantial. In reality, as far as its stable value is concerned, a piece of money is as flexible as a rubber band.

To illustrate: suppose bread is sold at $1 per loaf. Your dollar would be worth $1 as far as a loaf of bread is concerned. Now, imagine bread rising in price to $2 per loaf. Your dollar is now only worth half a loaf of bread, even though neither the bread itself nor your dollar have changed. This applies to the purchase of everything. The strength of your dollar depends entirely upon the value that is placed on the commodity you buy.

Suppose there are 10 people in a room and only one person has any money, just $1. We'll call him Man #1.

- Man #2 has a pocketknife he's willing to sell to Man #1 for $1. Man #1 buys it, giving his dollar to Man #2.

- Man #3 has a book that Man #2 wants. Man #2 gives his dollar to Man #3.

- This goes on until finally Man #10 has the dollar, and even he doesn't keep it. He buys something from Man #1 for a $1. In this room, ten dollars' worth of cash transactions took place with only $1 in actual currency.

This same principle applies in commerce. In the United States, many, many billions of dollars change hands each year, with only a fraction of the amount in real currency.

Gold is something that seems to have intrinsic value, yet the worth placed on gold is manmade. It's not decreed by nature. It rises and falls according to current financial and political situations operating in the world at any particular time.

The U.S. dollar used to be backed by gold, but after 1971, it was turned into *fiat money*, which means that the currency is no longer backed by gold but represents the services and products of the country. Gold-backed money was inefficient for a growing economy. Now, the value of money is created by what people perceive it to be.

It's not my intention to enter into a discussion of economics. I just want to make a point regarding the unreality of money. If you've followed the reasoning given so far, you'll agree money is not a material thing at all, but rather a means of exchange based on a nationally accepted idea.

The only thing money ever really pays for is labor. Think about the food you buy. Nature provides that food free of charge. The cost comes from the labor involved in growing the crops, transporting the foodstuffs and selling it in the grocery store.

We now reach the conclusion that the only thing we can buy with money is labor, and the value of labor isn't stable. Fifty years ago, if you had $10,000 saved up, you could make the down payment on a substantial home and have enough money remaining to make an initial payment on the furnishings. Today, you can't even get a standard mortgage without a 10 to 20 percent down payment, and this doesn't include closing costs.

## The Concept of Ownership

Now that you understand how limited money really is, think about what it's used for—to buy things we will then own. But, ask yourself this: "Do I really own anything?" The reality is that *none of us own anything*.

You may be very proud of your home ownership, but do you truly own it? If you hold a mortgage, the mortgage company really owns the property; they even hold the deed. You're nothing but a glorified renter.

What if you owe no mortgage on that same home? There are still taxes to be paid. Fail to pay that hefty bill and you won't own your home for long.

The same is true for most of your big-ticket possessions. There is always some other fee associated with their upkeep, and if you don't pay those fees, the item is taken from you. Look around your home. Of all of the things you "own," how many of them are truly and completely yours?

The grounds surrounding my home are beautifully landscaped and present the appearance of a small, well-kept park. Are they mine? They are, as long as I maintain them and don't allow them to become overrun with weeds. Likewise, you may have an extensive wardrobe, yet the garments are continually wearing out and going out of style.

Even the lumber in your house is affected by the weather and can be destroyed by termites. Without constant repair and renewal, your house would disintegrate into a valueless mass.

*In this life, we own nothing.* We have the use of various items as long as we pay our taxes and care for them.

What have we learned so far — and what good will this knowledge do for us? We've learned money buys nothing but labor, and the amount of labor our dollars will buy depends upon the value placed upon labor.

We've also learned that in this life, we own nothing but merely have use of material things. In fact, we don't even own our bodies. They are loaned to us and how long we keep them depends upon the care we give them.

As soon as one realizes money is a means to an end and not the end itself. It's established as a convenient means for barter, then it is easier to gain a broader perspective on the many facets of life.

A worker, in reality, is not working for the money he or she receives on payday. The worker is working for food, clothes and shelter. The money provides a handy means of evaluating the commodities and services he or she buys. Once you understand that, it is easier to work with your money.

## Redefining Material Goals

What do you really want to accomplish with the money you have—and plan to have in the future? Hoarding dollars in the bank isn't useful. Your subconscious mind needs something to work with. Determine what you want to do with your increased wealth. Keeping your mind on what you *want* forces your subconscious mind to *guide* you in thought and action to attain your objectives.

Here's an interesting fact: if you concentrate on just obtaining more money, you will limit your subconscious mind and find that you amass wealth at a much lower rate. However, if you become enthusiastically excited about buying a new home, your subconscious mind, with its reasoning faculties, will show you ways to save the money needed to buy that house. Your mind needs a goal to work toward, not just a command to do something or amass more dollar bills.

The subconscious mind needs to achieve. Accomplishment is more than simply earning additional dollars. Think of some of the greatest men and women in history. While they may have amassed great wealth, their achievements are what make them stand out:

**Henry Ford:** Few people think only of Ford's wealth. Instead they credit him with implementing the assembly line and giving the average person the ability to own an automobile.

**Bill Gates:** This Harvard dropout revolutionized home computing. While his wealth is widely covered, few people think about it when powering up their PC or laptop.

**Charles Lindbergh:** A man of considerable means, yet what does his name mean to you? You think of him as the man who pioneered transatlantic aviation.

**Walt Disney:** Disney was a film producer, screenwriter and entrepreneur. He made his dreams into a reality with the production of feature-length animated films and the creation of Disneyland and Walt Disney World. We think of him in connection with his visionary films and theme parks but not the money he made in producing them.

It's not their bank accounts that set these people apart. It is their deeds and how their actions impacted life for the rest of us. Of course, it was also those deeds that created the wealth they were able to enjoy for the rest of their lives. Think about your own goals. Is it money you want, or is the money just the way for you to get what you *really* want? Once you can differentiate between the two, you will be in a better position to guide your subconscious mind so it can lead you to exactly what you want.

# Seven: Your Consciousness and Your Wealth

How much wealth is enough? Ask this question to 10 different people in 10 different stages of life, and you'll get 10 very different answers. The teenager may say that $1,000 would make him feel rich, while the young executive in his 20s may admit that $25,000 for a new car would make him feel rich. The married couple in their 40s may answer the question by saying, "When our house is paid for, we have enough saved to pay for our children's education and sufficient funds put away for retirement, that's when we'll feel rich." And the retired couple enjoying good health and freedom in their schedules may say, "We're already rich." Meanwhile, the millionaire may worry when his portfolio dips below a certain amount, even though that amount is a thousand times what the average American ever dreams of accumulating. Wealth is relative. It all depends on who you are, what you already have and what you want.

It's doubtful that someone who looks at $5,000 as being a lot of money could ever fathom him- or herself a millionaire. He or she may envy the millionaire and wish for riches but can't envision him- or herself ever owning that amount of money. On the other hand, the individual with a million-dollar bank account thinks of $1,000 as pocket change.

The way you look at money is what changes your perspective. It's a matter of consciousness. One key to financial success is developing a financial consciousness that allows you to see yourself with the amount of money you now only dream of having.

How can the average person gain this type of prosperity consciousness? It takes reaching the point at which you can see yourself having the amount of money you want. This doesn't mean wishing you were a millionaire; it means visualizing yourself as a millionaire. Stop looking at your financial situation as a lost cause. No matter where you are right now—in debt, living paycheck to paycheck, etc.—you can train your mind to know and believe you can become prosperous. Until you reach that point, real wealth will always be just beyond your grasp.

I don't think there's a stronger motivating force than having a great desire for something you don't possess. When you see something in a shop window or in an ad that you really must have, you'll soon find your constructive imagination working out ways and means of obtaining it once you reach the point where you can actually see yourself enjoying it.

## *What Are You Worth?*

How much are you really worth? Consider this question carefully. Just because your paycheck lists a value for a week's worth of your time, that doesn't mean you're really worth that amount. Maybe you're worth more than the sum total in your weekly paycheck, or maybe you're worth less. Either way, it's an amount assigned to you by someone else. You may have accepted it, but that doesn't mean you *believe* it.

Whatever number you come up with, it is your invisible price tag. You carry this amount around in your head all day long whether you realize it or not, and it dictates how you do your job and how you respond to opportunities that arise.

Maybe your current job pays $45,000 a year, but you think you're worth $75,000. Two things may be the result:

1. You work harder to create the same value in the mind of your employer and get a promotion or pay raise.

2. You begin slacking off because you think you're being taken advantage of.

Which way will you respond to the disparity you find between the amount of money your employer pays you and what you think you're worth? The smart person decides to increase their perceived value by doing more work, being smarter on the job and giving their employer much more than what's expected.

Now that you see how to make a connection between what you think you're worth and the amount of your actual paycheck, it's possible to increase your income by simply increasing your invisible price tag.

I tried this experiment at a recent sales seminar. I challenged each participant to double their invisible price tag when they returned to the sales floor, but that wasn't all. I also told them to make plans to raise their standard of living to meet that figure. Whether it meant buying a new home, car or even an RV, they were to plan for getting that particular item within a specific amount of time—you know, as if the money were already in the bank.

I checked back with the sales manager three months later, and guess what I discovered? All but two of the seminar's participants had doubled or tripled their sales during that period of time, thus increasing their income substantially. What about the two who hadn't? Well, they'd been very vocal after leaving the seminar about how stupid my request had been and hadn't even tried the strategy. It's too bad for them because their coworkers are now enjoying larger incomes and the benefits of all the extra cash.

Does it mean you're poor because you're thinking yourself poor? Maybe. Riches are a matter of consciousness. If you expect to simply scrape by in life, never anticipating much more than an average paycheck, that's exactly what you're going to get. You have to want a better life to get one. No one's going to hand it to you unless you deserve it, and you won't deserve it until you think you do. Allow your subconscious mind to believe wealth can be yours and begin taking the plans necessary to obtain riches. Then, you will get them. Sound impossible? The mind offers great power. This fable illustrates the difference between negative and positive thinking:

Henry John was a strong man of excellent health, but one who had never been a success in life. He always envied other men of means but could never see himself so blessed.

John Henry, on the other hand, was a wealthy man, but he never had very good health. He was often treated for one illness or another. He always envied people with robust health.

A world-famous surgeon came to town, a man who claimed he could take two men and, through surgery, exchange their brains, taking one man's brain and putting it in the other man's head, and vice versa.

John Henry and Henry John got together and agreed to exchange brains. This would mean that Henry John would trade his healthy body for John Henry's wealth and unhealthy body.

The operation took place and for a while appeared to be very successful. John Henry, now a poor man, had been so accustomed to thinking in terms of wealth, in no time at all he accumulated another fortune. At the same time, however, as in the past, he began thinking of all the aches and pains he'd had before. It was not long before he began developing aches and pains in his new body.

Henry John, now a wealthy man, had always thought of himself as poor. Through unwise investments and foolish spending, he soon spent all the fortune he'd gained through the exchange of brains. On the other hand, he hadn't thought of his body as being sickly and, because he never brooded about physical ailments and understood the power of exercise, his body soon became as strong and vigorous as the one he had traded to the wealthy man. In time, both men returned to their original conditions. The former wealthy man again became wealthy. The former impoverished man again became poor.

Of course, life isn't a Disney movie and people can't exchange brains, but the lessons in this fable are still true. Your thinking and self-image make you what you are. In attempting to understand that one must have a consciousness of prosperity to become wealthy, don't think miracles will happen. Seeing yourself as being wealthy without putting any corresponding effort in doesn't mean you'll magically become rich. As you learned earlier, your subconscious mind, with its reasoning faculties, will *guide* you, in thought and action, to think the thoughts and do the things to bring about the success you're after.

## The Wealth Opportunities in Your Brain

Who wouldn't want to think themselves rich? Not only does the concept sound easy, it sounds fun. However, is it really possible? If you've read the whole book to this point and tried some of the exercises, I suspect you know it is, and now I will teach you exactly how to do it.

There's an old proverb that says, "Seek thy comrades among the industrious for the idle will sap the energy from thee."

In more modern phrasing, that proverb reads, "Find associates who are hard-working because lazy people suck out your energy." The proverb tells you to focus your energy on people and things that will add to your success and steer clear of energy vampires. Now, I don't mean using people to move ahead in life. What I'm saying is that certain people invigorate us and give us energy to strive for more while others simply drain us and make us wonder what the purpose of all that work is anyway. Don't fall prey to these vampires. Spend time with those who can see your vision and give you the support and energy to keep moving forward toward your quest for prosperity. It will make it so much easier to get to work, which is good. It's hard work and diligence coupled with the right thought process that will get you where you want to be.

## Three Steps to an Abundant Life

Changing your thoughts and attitude, surrounding yourself with the right kind of people and getting to work are all important steps toward tapping into the power of the subconscious mind and developing a whole new world for yourself. However, there are three more things you need to do to achieve the kind of success you're after:

1. **Ask**: Know what you want, and then clearly ask the universe for it. Hazy thinking won't result in much success.

2. **Believe**: You must truly see yourself as being who you want to be and/or having what you want. If you don't believe it's possible to obtain the wealth and success you're after, how will anyone else believe you're capable of it, either?

3. **Receive**: You have to put yourself in a state of *receiving* to allow the objects of your desires to come to you. How do you do that? Let your subconscious mind work on receiving while you sleep. Give yourself the suggestion before bed, and let your mind do the work.

All of these steps take one thing you might not be ready to trust: *imagination*. Scores of self-improvement books are built around this word. "One must imagine him- or herself as a success," the authors write. Sadly, many readers answer this calling with the statement, "But I have no imagination." If you're one of those people, get ready to change your mind — everyone has imagination, even though many don't realize it.

Imagination is that ability to envision reality differently. One possessed with *constructive* imagination will see current or future reality as he or she *wants* it to be. One with *negative* imagination sees things as he or she *fears* they will be.

Every individual is capable of using imagination, both constructively and negatively. Luckily, since you're in control of your own thoughts, you can choose which path to take.

I think one of the reasons why so many people have trouble raising their sights very high above their present circumstances is that the contrast between what they have and what they would like to have seems too great. For example, if your bank account is down to its last $50, it would seem utterly impossible to imagine you could build that account to $1,000,000 in your lifetime. Let's throw all of that aside and do a little imagining.

What would you do if someone offered you a job with an initial salary of only a penny the first month, but with the understanding this figure would double each month for a period of three years? You'd probably laugh at the offer and walk away. But since this is taking place in our imagination, let's do the math before we chuckle. Start with the number 1 and double it; then keep on doubling the sum 36 times. For example: 1-2-4-8-16-32, etc. Do the math. You'll be stunned to learn that if you had taken the job, your very last paycheck after three years would've been $1,372,796,089.60. Did you realize that 1¢ could grow to such a fabulous figure in such a short time? It takes very little to start a great fortune. In fact, it takes just a single penny.

I don't suggest you take a job paying just a penny the first month. What I do suggest is that $1,000,000 isn't as far off as you might think. Stop thinking about the large end result and start thinking in small incremental steps that will get you there. The journey to riches is not as overwhelming as you might think. The key is taking the individual steps to build it.

Kendall was a young woman with a dream. She loved old Victorian houses and dreamed of owning one someday. She scoured home magazines drooling over the beautiful renovated palaces, fearing she would never be able to afford one of the grand homes. Then, she came up with an idea. Why wait? Why couldn't she buy an old rundown home and renovate it herself?

It wasn't long before she found just what she was looking for on a short sale. Well, sort of what she was looking for—frankly, the house was a mess. Her friends and family thought she was nuts and would lose everything she'd invested. Kendall had a plan though. First, she took classes at her local technical school for electricity and plumbing. Then, she attended every free workshop her local home improvement store offered. There she learned how to sand and repair hardwood flooring, install tiles, repair a leaky roof and even check for mold in the basement.

It took a few years and a lot of hard work, but soon the house was in great shape. She lived in it for a few months, and then someone approached her with an offer to buy it. She was about to walk away when the person threw out a number to begin negotiations. Kendall stopped, stunned. The buyer was offering her three times what the house and renovations had cost— and this was her first attempt at flipping. She took the offer and bought herself another old house to renovate.

Having much more knowledge this time around, she was able to offer more period-appropriate touches to the next house and before long, she was known as the historic renovator in her community. Whether someone wanted to restore the house they already lived in or wanted to buy a Victorian style that was already finished, they contacted Kendall.

Then, something amazing happened. A popular home repair channel heard about her restoration of vintage homes and offered her a television series. Now she shows millions of viewers how to restore vintage homes to their former glory. At 33, she enjoys work that she loves, popularity she never dreamed of and riches beyond her imagination—all because she had the guts to think she could learn how to renovate an old house.

If Kendall can step beyond her perceived limitations and go after her dream, why can't you? It doesn't matter how big or small your dream is or how much wealth you're after, you can have everything you want—if you choose to believe.

# Eight

# Drawing Power from Contrasts

I have a friend who absolutely loves living in the northeast part of the country. I'm a warm weather person myself. I love climates that remain the same all year long. Not my friend. He loves feeling the chill of an icy morning, the warm breeze of spring, the heat and humidity of summer, and the brisk cool down of fall. He's a man of contrasts. "If every day looks and feels the same, I'd be bored and fail to appreciate the good things around me," he often remarks. I must admit he has a point. When you wake every morning to the same view and the same weather, it can be easy to lose sight of the wonderfulness around you. Winters are hard here in Ohio, but I wouldn't trade them for the world because they help me appreciate all the other amazing seasons we get to enjoy.

## Why You Need Contrast

Contrast adds zest to life. It's something to be relished, not pushed aside and forgotten. Have you ever been sick? I mean really, really sick? Maybe you were in the hospital, unable to eat or even get out of bed. Once you were out of the woods and finally on the mend, you probably dreamt of all the wonderful meals you'd have when you were fully recovered or the long walks you'd take in the park when you were finally out of bed. The illness you'd endured was bad, maybe even horrible, but it gave you a new perspective. It allowed you to see the contrast between the good and the bad in your life. Without this type of contrast, life becomes boring and mundane.

I remember when I was hospitalized at the Cleveland Clinic. As I recovered post surgery, it was the little changes that made the biggest difference—the sweet taste of juice after nothing but water for days, the ability to walk outside after weeks in bed. The colors seemed brighter, the smells stronger. Life just seemed to have this extra dimension that had been missing for so long.

Don't let contrast scare you. Instead, embrace it. No, do more than that—plan for it. Let's say you grew up in a moderate middle-class home. Now suppose that by following the principles outlined in this book, you build a fortune enabling you to live in luxury for the rest of your life. If you do nothing beyond making the fortune, the money would eventually become meaningless because there would be no contrast. However, if you lay out a long-range, step-by-step program, extended for many years, you could assure yourself continuous satisfaction.

## Designing Your Life

Your first step may be to get your financial house in order by either adjusting your expenses in accordance with your income or increasing your income to meet your expenses.

The next step could be to arrange a portfolio of investments so you could accumulate a backlog of savings to ensure future security. Then, begin buying the stuff you've always dreamed of owning: a big house, great cars, etc.

Once you get the stuff you were after, look for new trails to blaze. After your accumulated wealth is sufficient to give you and your family all that you require, you'll be ready for the thrill of your lifetime—helping others—those who genuinely deserve your help.

Keeping contrast alive in your life will keep your days from becoming mundane and boring. Plus it will always give you something to work toward: first amassing your fortune, then spending some of it, and finally helping others.

## *Using Contrasts to Get What You Want*

Life offers some abundant blessings but it can also present some real hardships. It's how you handle those hardships that either make or break you. Too many people spend their days feeling sorry for themselves. They allow self-pity and doubt to erode their confidence and keep them in place they'd rather not be.

"Why do people feel sorry for themselves?" I often ask myself. It's amazing how many times self-pity stems from a lack of contrast. An individual will be living under some sort of adverse condition and instead of taking steps to change it, he or she pities him- or herself for what he or she must deal with. If only individuals like this realized that, within their power, they possess the means to change their circumstances. If they did, they'd see their current reality as nothing more than a challenge offered to their subconscious.

Jill was a single mother with two boys. Her latest boyfriend had just moved out, and she was stuck at a dead-end waitressing job. Jill dragged herself into work day after day, rarely smiling or being pleasant to anyone, including her customers. Life was hard, and she showed the world just how hard.

One day, a customer asked her why she always looked so glum. She said, "What do I have to be happy about? I have a crummy job, a crummy apartment, two kids and my boyfriend just left me."

Her customer smiled gently. "Are your children healthy?"

"Yes," she answered.

"Do you have enough food to feed them?"

"Yes," Jill replied.

"Do you make enough to buy what you and your kids need?"

"Yes."

The customer smiled and said, "Then what don't you have to be happy about? Maybe if you smiled once in awhile, you'd earn even more and invite a different class of people into your social circle."

At first Jill scoffed at what said the customer said, but as the day wore on, she began wondering. *What would happen if I smiled more and concentrated on what I have instead of what I don't?*

For the rest of that day, she smiled at customers, indulged in chitchat and was just plain nice. She was surprised to see her tips were double at the end of her shift. She then went home and began making the most out of all the good things she had. Instead of looking at

2

her rundown apartment as a curse, she went out the next day and bought a can of paint and repainted the living room wall a bright, happy yellow. Her kids loved it. Then, she began spending time playing games with her kids at night. Soon, they were relaxed and better behaved, which made her calmer all day long, especially at work. Life seemed to be getting better for her.

About a month later, the same customer came into the restaurant. "You're smiling!" he said. "So what has changed in your life? Did you get a new job? A new apartment? A new boyfriend?"

Jill answered no to all three questions. "I just decided to stop feeling sorry for myself." She chuckled.

"And how is that working out for you?" he asked.

"Wonderfully," she said with a smile. Best of all—she meant it.

To instantly improve your life and master yourself, spend time being happy about who you are and where you are in life. Instead of feeling sorry for yourself, accept your present circumstances as they are, as a foundation upon which to build. Take all the negative elements that disturb you and, one by one, make yourself see them as positives. Do you see what this accomplishes? It forces you to develop a series of contrasts that will open up new vistas of happiness for you.

A few years ago, during the Great Recession, an associate of mine named Bill called upon a prospect who needed to order medical supplies.

The prospect, making conversation, said, "How's business?"

"Horrible," Bill whined.

The prospect, a successful executive, shook his head and said, "You do realize you can change your business, right? In fact, you're the one making it horrible in the first place."

Bill looked shocked, but his customer went on. "Don't look at me like that—you can take this. Your job is to make me want to buy from you, right? Well, how in the hell do you think you can inspire anyone to spend money when you come in with a face like a zombie and nothing but negativity coming out of your mouth?"

"I know you're right, but I can't tell someone business is good when we both know it's not," Bill replied.

"You're working hard to get business, right?" asked the customer.

"Well, yes," Bill answered.

"Then, when prospects ask how business is, tell them you're busier than you've ever been. It's the truth, and you make your products seem even more attractive. When you say business is horrible, it doesn't make me feel bad for you—it makes me wonder what's wrong with your merchandise, and that won't help your sales."

Bill left the meeting and, with some reluctance, decided to incorporate this advice into his routine. He called upon a second prospect just before lunch. When asked about business, he told the prospect he had never been busier in his life.

"Come out to lunch with me," was the unexpected reply. "It's good to spend an hour with a doer instead of listening to one hard-luck story after another."

The two had a pleasant lunch together, and when they returned to the office, the customer gave Bill the biggest order he had ever received.

How did Bill land such a big order in such a stale economy? It was the contrast between Bill's approach to one simple question and the approach of those who'd whined and complained about business. Bill's friendly, optimistic attitude put the prospect in a buying mood, instead of making him feel he'd better conserve every cent.

It's true there are two sides to every story. It's also true that opportunity lies within every condition. If something doesn't suit you as it is, instead of trying to grin and bear it, look for a contrast. Look for the condition that would be ideal for you; then, apply the principles you've learned to attain the improvement you desire.

# Nine:

# Dozing, Dreaming, Prospering

Your body needs sleep. It's during this restful state that the cells of your body regenerate and fix all sorts of problems. Even precancerous cells can be destroyed during sleep—meaning sleep is literally a lifesaver.

The same is true for the subconscious mind. While it doesn't sleep, it does use sleep as a way to plan. It's during sleep that the creative part of your subconscious mind rids itself of bad thoughts that can sabotage your daytime efforts for success and replaces them with constructive thoughts and plans.

Have you ever noticed that even the worst problems seem much less harrowing after a good night's sleep?

Or that foggy, hazy, unsure thinking is suddenly crystal clear after a short nap? Sleep gives the subconscious mind time to sort through problems and come up with answers you already have but that your conscious brain has difficulty accessing.

One of the main ways the subconscious mind works while you sleep is by moving information to the conscious mind as needed. Like a handyman who only brings to the job the tools needed to complete his work, the conscious mind only extracts the information it needs. Unless the subconscious mind floods the conscious mind with the information it wants, the conscious mind can't remember and use it.

The conscious mind is very good at grabbing stored facts but also at finding new ones that exist outside your brain in reference books, videos, websites and other information sources when needed. However, the subconscious mind can only use the facts you already know and have stored in your memory. These facts are also stored not just objectively, but with a positive or negative tint based on your overall attitude. This sometimes can make the decisions and plans presented by the unconscious mind faulty, especially when the information is negative in nature. Therefore, it's important to take on a positive attitude.

Suppose you have the opportunity to buy into a new franchise. You can't decide what to do, so before you go to bed, you summon your creative mind to mull over the question during your resting time. Now, if your subconscious mind is full of negative thoughts and facts, your answer in the morning will likely be "No, I'd better not take on this business." On the other hand, if your creative mind has been stuffed with positive thoughts, it's much more likely to decide to take on the new challenge, with the resolve and ability to make it a success.

Now you understand why it's so important to keep telling yourself you can be successful. Until it develops an impenetrable layer of positivity, even your subconscious mind can work against you.

## Empowering the Subconscious

Suppose your house needs a new roof. You call an experienced roofer, let him tell you what needs done, and let him do it. You don't doubt his ability to be on the new roof. You feel confident the roofer knows what he is doing and will get the job completed on schedule. It's possible to give our subconscious mind instructions with the same certainty: the task you give it will be completed.

Remember, your subconscious works best when your conscious is in either neutral (asleep) or pleasantly occupied. When you have a big decision to make, you can do two things to help your creative mind mull it over:

1. Ask your subconscious to find an answer while you sleep.

2. Keep yourself busy doing something less mentally taxing such as sailing, gardening or enjoying a quiet walk while your creative mind works on the problem subconsciously.

Writers have used this tactic for years. When writer's block hits and she gets stuck, a colleague of mine goes to her backyard and hits tennis balls against her garage. Another writer friend likes to fish and yet another explains that weeding his garden always seems to break the block. It isn't the exercise that helps clear away the cobwebs; it's the break that allows their creative minds to work out the problem at hand.

Robert Updegraff, in his book, *Putting Your Subconscious Mind to Work for You,* said, "It's not so much a lack of Brain Power or of business capacity or acumen that keeps people from progressing faster toward their objectives, and toward a solid position in the world. It's rather because they take only half a mind into business with them. The result is that they work their conscious mind too hard, too many hours of the day, and too many days of the year. We feel virtuous, because we work so hard and so conscientiously that we are tired, whereas we should feel ashamed that we work so hard, and make so little progress, and we are weary of mind."

What Mr. Updegraff means by "half a mind" is that we attempt to do all of our work *consciously* without taking advantage of the tremendous reservoir of power at our command in the subconscious.

Start forming the habit of putting the subconscious mind to work *for* you right now. Its power is limitless. To be successful, it's essential to take more time for enjoyable diversion and rest instead of working harder and longer. This works for two reasons:

1. Your subconscious mind, if permitted to, will direct you in your work, making it better, easier to perform and far more pleasant.

2. You can, at will, direct your subconscious to assist you in the solving of problems, to help you make the right decisions and create ways and means toward great achievement.

Are you ready to get your subconscious mind on your road to success? Here are some practical tips to get you started:

1. **Understand that your subconscious mind can work for or against you.** It's best to fill it with the positive thoughts, feelings and facts it will need to do the most good.

2. **Be specific in the instructions you give your subconscious mind.** If it's better health you want, *know* that your subconscious mind is directing the glands and organs of your body to bring you better health, and thoughts will enter your consciousness directing you to do the things necessary to promote better health.

If you desire further advancement in your work, *know* that your subconscious mind will direct you to take the steps necessary to assure advancement.

3. **Know that your subconscious mind, with its reasoning faculties, will provide a practical solution for you.** Your subconscious mind stands ready, able and willing to assist you in any way you desire.

4. **State your instructions to your subconscious mind in positive form.** Say, "I *will* be successful in my new business," rather than, "I will *not* fail in my new business." Your subconscious mind will ignore the negative word and give you what you've asked for in the rest of the sentence.

5. **Free your mind from worry.** Worry prevents you from doing the things that can actually prevent you from ever having to worry. To worry is to doubt the intelligence and power of your subconscious mind. Instead, devote the time you might use for worry to find constructive ways to plan a way of overcoming the problem.

6. **Actively visualize your results.** Don't just wish for better conditions through your subconscious mind;

*visualize* your perfect circumstances. Sense the feeling of *self-mastery* that comes when you fully understand the truth of the statement made earlier, to the effect that *the conscious mind is the master, the subconscious mind the servant.*

Now, let's take these practical steps a bit further, developing a plan for success. This magic formula can be used to focus on how to get rich while you sleep. Follow these four rules to gain the full cooperation of your subconscious mind:

1. Before going to sleep, relax thoroughly, both mentally and physically. Meditation can help you relax.

2. Think of your problem. Think it through. Think of your subconscious mind as the best personal assistant in the world. You explain what you'd like to have done and then rest in the knowledge that your assistant will accomplish it perfectly.

3. Believe in your success. If you've developed faith in your subconscious mind, it's easy to have a

successful attitude. You *know* it's able, ready and willing to serve you.

4. After you've gone this far, remove all thoughts of the problem from your conscious mind, knowing the solution will be forthcoming at the right time. In other words, don't dwell on it.

Let's say, for example, that you're offered two different jobs from two different companies. They're both excellent opportunities, and you can't decide which one to take. Call upon your subconscious mind for the answer. Go through each of the steps above, and then go to sleep, knowing that in the morning you'll have an answer. The next morning, you'll awaken and find thoughts coming into your consciousness that will help guide you. With this knowledge will be the reasons why you should go in a certain direction or why you should avoid it. The succession of ideas will be so logical you won't be able to doubt it. That's how the subconscious mind works—while you're asleep. So forget the sleepless nights worrying about what decision to make. Go to sleep, peaceful in the knowledge that when you wake, your decision will be made—and it will be the right one for you.

# Ten:

# Accepting the Power of Thought

Think about all the times you've failed in your life and the times you've succeeded. What made the difference? It's very likely it was the way you thought about your plan, which affected what you did.

I have this friend, Mary, who gained a lot of weight while pregnant with her second child. Unhappy with the way she looked, she decided to lose those extra pounds within six months of her son's birth. She not only decided to do just that, but she also visualized what she would look like. She knew it was possible. You know what? In fewer than six months, she was 14 pounds lighter than she had been when she became pregnant.

Now, fast-forward 15 years. This same friend began having medical issues and had to have surgery. Her doctors told her the medications would likely make her gain some weight, and coupled with her inactivity as she healed, she indeed gained 30 pounds. Now this time, everyone she talked to warned her that her medical condition plus her age would make it hard to lose the pounds. She began believing what they said.

She kept telling herself, hoping to ward off any disappointment if she failed to lose weight, "My metabolism is slower than it has been in the past, and I'm still taking this medication, so I guess I won't lose as much." Do you know what happened? She gained 10 more pounds.

That was two years ago. When I saw Mary last week, she looked great. She was back to her pre-baby size and looked healthier than she had in years. I asked her how she did it. She said, "I took your advice and changed my attitude! Instead of giving myself all those excuses for not losing the weight, I started asking my subconscious mind how I could do it. Each day I was surprised at new ideas for cutting calories, exercising more and just enjoying the process. The pounds suddenly started melting away!"

Mary is just one example of how accepting the power of your own thoughts can help you accomplish your goals. There are dozens of additional examples from which you can learn. Begin noticing those in your neighborhood or industry who seem to make it. What made them stand out from all the others who tried but failed at their quest?

## *Visualizing Your Future*

Some of you reading this book will be tempted to think you can jump from mediocrity to mega success in a single leap—or after a single night's sleep. It's not impossible. For some people, just the briefest introduction into positive thought makes an immediate and grand difference, but they are the outliers. Most people need time to grow from the conception to believing. There's much to learn along the way, so take time to discover the skills necessary to succeed. There's no question you will begin feeling happier pretty quickly, but you may not have significant changes in your lifestyle that create this happiness—you'll just begin interpreting life differently.

Instead of attempting to open a 12-franchise business overnight, open a single store in a popular neighborhood. Learn what it takes to make that one store a success, and then open the next one... and the next one... and the next. Not only does this strategy make more sense, it's also more fun. Imagine accomplishing your entire dream in a short period of time. What's the fun and excitement in that? Instead, enjoy the ride and give yourself time to get the most out of the journey.

Anticipation is greater than realization, or so the old saying goes. Taking the journey is always more exhilarating than reaching your destination. Enjoy every twist and turn along the way. That, after all, is the fun part.

## *Your Mind versus Your Brain*

Your mind and your brain are not the same thing. The brain acts as a receiving station for the thoughts and ideas that get there through your mind. The brain can become damaged or sick, but your mind cannot. It's capable of achieving great things, no matter who you are. The trick is re-educating both your conscious and subconscious mind to hold positive and creative thoughts.

Re-educating your mind isn't always a simple task. It requires diligence. Once you decide you're going to rid your mind of negative chatter and fill it with positive thoughts, you'll know you can accomplish the goal at hand. That knowledge will spark your subconscious mind to direct your conscious mind to tackle the job with a success-filled spirit. Before you know it, you'll begin experiencing small successes.

Every victory proves your ability to overcome even the most difficult situations. You'll have to work at it, but every time you attempt something new and succeed, you'll prove to your conscious mind you're capable of anything. The concept of "can't" will begin to fade from your thought process. Before long, you'll think exclusively in terms of CAN and WILL.

Each of us has the power within our minds to change our direction and future. All we must do is tap into our subconscious mind and allow it to figure out a solution to our problems. Every time you solve a problem, you'll learn what to do and never struggle with that particular dilemma again.

You may think you want a life totally free of problems, but that would be boring for both your brain and your mind. Problems are a way for us to learn and challenge ourselves to rise to the occasion and grow. Our problems aren't what bother us. It's the underlying lack of faith we have that we'll be able to solve them. Boost your faith and face your problems head-on. Write down the phrase below on a small card and carry it with you. Before going to bed, read it over once or twice. When you wake up in the morning, you'll have peace in knowing you have what it takes to solve any problem that comes your way.

*I am at peace with myself and the world.*

*I am no longer afraid of the problems I may face because I know I have the intelligence and power to solve them.*

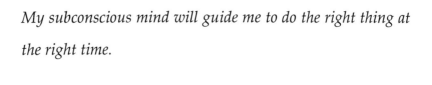
## Designing Your Life

*My subconscious mind will guide me to do the right thing at the right time.*

# Eleven: The Importance of Mental and Physical Exercise

Our population is aging. With age comes experience, but all too often those who have the most to offer allow their minds to atrophy, becoming too indecisive to be taken seriously, let alone accomplish great things.

Just because your body begins slowing down at a certain age doesn't mean your mind must do the same. Look at, billionaire businessman, Warren Buffet. Well into normal retirement age, Buffet is as sharp as ever, constantly challenging younger folks to keep up both in the business and political worlds. An intelligent man with years of business experience behind him, he is just one example of how to keep the mind sharp, despite the number of candles on his birthday cake.

Maybe you're nowhere near those retirement years. Does that mean you don't have to work at keeping sharp? Not in the least. It doesn't matter whether you're 20, 40, 60 or 80, if you don't use your brain, it will atrophy.

## Understanding Frustration

It's easy to get frustrated these days. Schedules are so packed with things to do and places to go, our frustration levels seem to rise higher by the hour. Why else would people become so overwhelmed at other drivers on the road that they erupt in dangerous rage?

Frustration may be common, but it doesn't have to be. It's not a sign of taking on too much or even being overwhelmed. Frustration is a sign of an uncontrolled mind that has become panicked. When your mind is allowed to atrophy and begin experiencing times of ineptness and disorganization, it begins seeing problems where none exist.

The next time you feel completely overwhelmed and frustrated with your day, try this exercise:

> Write down every problem you feel is getting in your way. Most people can quickly jot down the first two. Then, it takes a few seconds to write down the third and a few more to figure out a fourth. By the time they reach number five on their list, they usually have to take more and more time to determine what problems really are standing in their way. Why? They don't have as many obstacles to overcome as they thought. It's just that their mind was so muddled with disorganized thoughts, they perceived their inability to sort through it all as being proof of having too much to handle. By writing down your problems, you can see how few you really have and give your mind the space to organize them and come up with solutions to each, one at a time. Suddenly, your frustrations will melt away.

## Remembering More and Forgetting Less

Forgetfulness is often caused by a disorganized mind. When the mind is in a state of turmoil, our powers of recall are lessened. Think of your conscious mind like a junk drawer. If you have no dividers or organization in your junk drawer, it'll be a nightmare to find anything. It's the same way with your mind.

When we wish to remember any fact in a disorganized mind, it's slow in coming. We accept the thought we are becoming forgetful and can actually grow more forgetful by encouraging that thought in our subconscious. The memories of those with well-disciplined minds are much keener than those with confused minds.

## A Treadmill for the Mind

Many people benefit from brainteasers, mental games and exercises designed to strengthen the mind power and encourage critical thinking. Most of the time, they think they're just having fun and letting off a little steam, but really, their minds are in basic training.

Any routine of exercises causing you to think is of value. You'll be amazed to find how quickly the mind responds and, in a very short time, you'll notice marked improvement in your ability to think quickly, logically and creatively.

While driving your car, you can do a fascinating exercise with the license plates on the cars ahead.

Take the license number and, by addition, reduce it to a single digit. This is done by adding all the digits together. If the result contains more than one digit, add those together. Keep this up until you've just one digit. Here are a few examples:

$978 = 9 + 7 + 8 = 24 = 2 + 4 = 6$

$164 = 1 + 6 + 4 = 11 = 1 + 1 = 2$

$899 = 8 + 9 + 9 = 26 = 2 + 6 = 8$

If the license plates have letters as well as numbers, you can make a game of the letters. In California, for example, the plates have three letters, such as PUD. As you see the letters, make up a person's name as fast as you can using those letters as initials. The name Patrick Ulrick Day may come to you as a name for the above letters. At first it will require a bit of thinking to make up names for the letters you see, but soon names will come to you almost as fast as you can mentally record the letters.

Sudoku, anagrams, quizzes and jumbles all stimulate the mind. Crossword puzzles not only add new words to your vocabulary but also exercise your skills of recall. As you continue working with them, you'll note that words come to your mind much faster than they did when you first took up the pastime.

Speed-reading is good practice. There are several methods of speed-reading from which to choose.

Reading faster also speeds your thinking and that, of course, sharpens your mind.

Dancing has been found to be one of the best mental stimulators ever. The combination of physical activity with having to learn and remember new steps is a winning combination.

Exercise in general helps a person's mental abilities. Getting all of the systems in the body active and encouraging vigorous blood flow helps your brain immeasurably.

## The Importance of Concentration

When you were a child, did you ever play with a magnifying glass, using it to focus the rays of the sun on a given object so enough heat was generated to cause a flame? You can do the same with the mind. When you learn to focus your thoughts without interference on a specific objective, it's astounding how much mental power you'll bring into being.

You can develop the powers of mental concentration through practice. The more you practice, the more fruitful the results will be.

A simple exercise is to see how long you can keep your thoughts on a single object. For example, light a candle, sit in front of it and see if you can keep your mind focused on it for five minutes. It sounds easy, but it isn't—it will take a lot of practice to master. You can think about any aspect of the candle you wish: the color, the scent or the heat coming from it.

After finishing your period of concentration, take a sheet of paper and write a brief journal entry on your experience. Do the same following every period of concentration. After a few weeks, compare these essays and note the improvement. Not only will you be improving your powers of observation, you'll also add to your ability to express yourself. It's not necessary to focus on a candle each time. Change to any item convenient to you: the television set, a lamp, your hat, etc.

Below are several questions relating to potential objectives you may have for your personal or professional life.

- How can I build a successful business?

- How can I get promoted in my present job?

- How can I afford the time and money to take an extended ocean voyage?

- How can I afford to live in a better home?

- How can I have perfect health?

- How can I find true love?

Take a sheet of paper and write down the one that appeals to you most. Think of yourself as a counselor and imagine a client has come to you with this question, and you're called upon to give a solution. Figure out what obstacles may get in the client's way of attaining each goal, and then develop a plan to help him or her overcome them.

First, use your conscious mind to come up with the answer to your chosen question. Take a sheet of paper and write down your answer in detail.

Next, go to bed with the same question in mind and allow your subconscious to work on it. In the morning, allow some time to write down the results. You'll be amazed at what your creative mind has come up with versus what your conscious mind did.

****

You may have thought any one of these questions were beyond practical answers. By the time you complete this module and have become accustomed to this exercise, you'll see marked results. With clear, logical, concentrated thinking, it won't be difficult to gain insight into your question.

Rhonda was a nurse's aide. When she entered the profession, she thought she could make a good living; yet she wasn't happy with her job. She didn't like the daily routine of patient care, but she never did anything about it except complain. She didn't think she had the intelligence and initiative to start a new career. She attended a lecture on mental improvement. The lecturer gave some mental exercises and, fortunately for Rhonda, the suggestions sank in. After she started to develop her mental faculties, she was even more dissatisfied with being a nurse's aide. The difference was that after doing these exercises she realized she was capable of doing something much more satisfying.

Rhonda always had an interest in new homes and loved the idea of decorating them. She stopped every time she saw an open house and began wondering why she couldn't become an interior designer. "Why can't I learn to decorate these homes?" she asked herself. With no negative reply ready, she started planning accordingly. She signed up for a few courses at her local community college and even began an online study of certain aspects of the job. Then, she started drawing up plans for different model homes in her area.

She arranged a meeting with a local builder to show him samples. By the end of the meeting, she was offered a contract position to decorate two of his new model homes. Those two jobs turned into two more. Today she works with multiple developers and private homeowners decorating individual rooms and entire estates.

Your mind can be a fountainhead of personal power and accomplishment. It's just a matter of learning to direct it. Put these exercises to use, and soon a new YOU will emerge. No longer will you envy others for their possessions and achievements because you'll know that if you want what they have, you can have it.

# Twelve: Choosing Pictures for Your Inner Scrapbook

Negative thoughts cause negative reactions. Positive thoughts cause positive reactions. We've explained this truth several times now, but why is it true? It's true because thoughts are transformed into pictures your mind can see. When you think a negative thought, your mind creates a negative image, which then transforms into negative feelings. The same is true for positive thoughts. It's these thought-pictures that create a pattern in your subconscious mind—a pattern that plays itself over and over again like a harp in your subconscious until it becomes your new reality. Hold a picture of failure in your mind, and failure is exactly what you'll encounter. Imagine success, and you will succeed.

Remember the movie, *Fireproof,* that hit theaters a few years ago? It was the story of a couple headed for divorce. They'd both become so disenchanted with their relationship they checked out, physically and emotionally. It wasn't until the husband began changing his mental pictures and attitude that things started improving.

He started by doing small things for his wife, like leaving her a cup of coffee in the morning or cleaning up his own messes in the kitchen. At first his efforts went unnoticed, but then she saw these small efforts as a sign of peace.

Things did not change outright, but slowly the pattern of resentment and selfishness was replaced with a pattern of selflessness and forgiveness. He was changing the loop in his own mind with small, otherwise insignificant actions, which was changing the loop in his wife's mind. It was these mental image changes that changed their attitudes toward one another and softened their hardened hearts.

You can do the same to accomplish any goal. Whether it's saving your marriage, getting out of debt or switching careers, a change in your mental photo album is a great step toward changing everything for the better.

## *Enthusiasm Adds Power to Positive Mental Film*

Developing mental pictures aimed at success is one thing, but what good is it when others are involved? After all, you can envision getting a promotion all you want, but unless an opportunity arises and your boss is willing to give you a try, that mental picture won't result in much. The key here is to use the power you have—your mental pictures—to influence the behavior of others.

I'm not referring to hypnosis or ESP here. It's much simpler than that. The key is enthusiasm. That's right, enthusiasm. When picture success and it's backed up by true enthusiasm, it prompts you to act in a way that will often be rewarded in a manner pleasing to you.

I'm not insinuating that by visualizing what you want, it will magically appear. However, by forming the right mental pictures, infusing them with deep emotion and believing in those images, your enthusiasm for what you want will soar, and you'll begin taking action on your desires. In short, those images will motivate you to do something. By doing something and appearing enthusiastic about your approach, others will begin believing in your capabilities and more opportunities will come your way.

Now, here's the tricky part: while positive mental pictures can make good things happen, negative ones can make bad things happen. The economy is tough right now, and jobs in some industries are scarce. If you constantly worry about losing your job, your performance at work will suffer, and you may indeed find yourself in the unemployment line.

## Drowning Out Doubt

Doubt is an insidious dream stealer. Even when trying to concentrate on only good messages, our subconscious mind can be invaded by doubt. The smallest doubt can ruin your plan for success. Be aware of any qualms you may have lingering in the back of your mind and squelch them immediately. No matter what you think may be hindering your success, find an alternative to the doubt and replant better images in your mind.

# Thirteen:
# The Vital Mental Eraser

Everyone wants a better memory, but sometimes the key to success is allowing yourself to forget. It's the memories of past hardships and difficulties that tend to discourage us. As we relive the fear and doubt of the past, we allow negative images to take hold in our subconscious, ruining our efforts at a better future.

Learning to erase the bad mental pictures of the past can be a good way to free yourself from the negativity that may hinder your success. Remember, we can learn important lessons from past failures so keep the memories, but get rid of the negative images held in your mind. Memories can be neutralized so they no longer contain power. Negative images, on the other hand, hold emotional baggage that needs to be erased.

Think of two business associates who worked at similar jobs in the real estate industry. When the housing bubble of 2008 popped, both were out of jobs, out of prospects and likely out of most of their savings. One man continued feeling sorry for himself and never recovered completely. He lost everything he owned and today works at a job he hates, making a fraction of what he did just 10 years ago.

The second associate understood there were plenty of people in the same situation. She studied the economy and made appropriate changes to reduce her debt. Although the real estate business went sour, she began looking at other ways to use her sales skills and real estate knowledge. It took a few years, but she now has a good job with a corporate relocation company. She helps clients find new homes when moving for work.

Not only can she help families find the right home, but she also has the insider information to help them strike a great deal. She loves her new job and is doing very well. Yes, she had to sell her multimillion-dollar home and two of her favorite cars, but basically her family and finances are intact. The rest she can rebuild as the economy improves.

So what was the difference between these two? One concentrated on the negative and the other learned from experience and used those memories to build more positive mental pictures to help overcome adversity and get back on track.

If you can, take your mental images and, like the second associate, rid yourself of the negative images and replace them with positive ones. Every time you think of something that causes a negative reaction, replace it with an image of something that brings you happiness and peace.

## *Thinking about Thinking*

In the following exercises, you'll begin *thinking about thinking*. This may sound strange at first, but as you *think about thinking*, you'll experience a great revelation. You'll begin seeing the gigantic reservoir of power you have at your command.

Become very critical about the thought pictures you allow to enter your mind. Each time you find a picture coming into consciousness that has any connection at all with failure, illness or gloom, remove it.

*Beware of wishful thinking.* To simply wish this book will help you gets you nowhere. You'll end up saying, "I read the book and didn't get a thing out of it," and it will be true. Things begin happening when you see them happening. This statement, of course, refers to good and bad things. If you see dire things happening, you're directing your powerful subconscious mind to make the pictures realities. Be thankful, however, that the reverse is true. When you see good things happening, you're directing your forces to make those pictures realities.

**\*\*\*\***

*Exercise 1:* When you're with a slacker, study his type of thinking. You'll invariably find his circumstances reflect his thinking. He thinks in terms of "I can't." He has all sorts of alibis about why he isn't doing any better than he is, and, unfortunately, in most cases he really believes his alibis are valid reasons instead of excuses.

*Exercise 2:* Spend a bit of time with a go-getter. Study her type of thinking. Instead of giving excuses, she shows results. She always looks for ways to master the situation and make it beneficial. Ask her where she gets her ideas. You'll find that often, her subconscious mind guides her in thought and action so she can solve problems.

## *Understanding the Structure of Positive Affirmations*

Bedtime is an excellent time to fill your mind with constructive pictures. Erase all pictures that have come into your mind because of the day's experiences. Go to bed with mental pictures of the *big* things that will happen the following day.

Here's a good formula to follow in creating mental pictures that will not react negatively:

*Picture the condition you want, not the condition you're attempting to overcome.*

To say "I won't fail" is negative. To say "I'm a success" is positive.

The thought "I won't get sick" is negative, whereas the expression "I have radiant health" is positive.

Suppose you're facing a situation so bad it's impossible to visualize the condition you want. As you try to form prosperous pictures of yourself, negative pictures keep creeping in. What now?

Instead of picturing yourself with your problems solved, hold pictures of yourself finding a solution to your problems. See yourself being guided to the proper things to overcome your problems. A surprise will be awaiting you when you awake. Before eating breakfast, ideas will pop into your consciousness telling you the things you can do to bring your problems to an end.

The extent of your success depends entirely upon the clarity of your mental pictures. If you can take your mental eraser and obliterate all pictures of doubt and inadequacy, and replace them with pictures showing the condition you would like to have, and if you have sufficient faith to know you can attain it, good things will begin happening.

# Fourteen: Building Your Mindset for Success

All achievement begins with thought. Knowing this fact is only part of the story. You can't use this strategy in your own life until you learn *how* to build a success mindset that allows you to see yourself as nothing but successful.

I once heard a story about two neighbors. One had an impressive home workshop, while the other didn't—but he did spend a lot of time watching his neighbor work in his. The neighbor without a workshop—we'll call him John—constantly reminded his neighbor Ed that he wasn't handy with tools, and he'd find it impossible to build the things Ed built.

One day, Ed took the time to prove John's insecurity wrong. He took the plans of a cabinet and literally dissected them. "This plan calls for six pieces of lumber 30 inches long, 12 inches wide and one inch thick. Could you take a board and cut it according to those dimensions?" Ed asked. Without hesitation, John admitted that he could. Then, Ed mentioned the size of other panels of the cabinet and asked John if he could cut those according to size. He said he could. On and on Ed went through each step, and John agreed that each would not be difficult.

The outcome of this experiment was that John borrowed some tools, went home and built a really good cabinet. Now he has a home workshop of his own replete with power tools. His home now shows evidence of his handiwork in every room. As soon as he gained a success consciousness regarding woodworking, he became proficient.

A success consciousness will lead you to success in any direction. If your desires include the building of an estate and financial security, a success consciousness will lead you there.

## Four Steps to Success

If you pause right now and reread this book before continuing further, you'd be able to write the formula for building a success consciousness. However, for your convenience, I'll give it to you here, step by step:

### Know You Can Accomplish Anything.

As a child, Amazon founder, Jeff Bezos, showed interest in how things work, turning his parents' garage into a laboratory and rigging electrical contraptions around his house. As a teenager, his family moved to Miami where he developed a love for computers and excelled in school, becoming the valedictorian of his class. In high school, he started his first business, the Dream Institute, an educational summer camp for fourth, fifth and sixth graders. Though he became extremely successful on Wall Street, he risked it all to venture into the new world of e-commerce. He startedAmazon.com, one of the most successful e-commerce sites in existence.

Did Jeff Bezos ever say, "I wonder if I can do this?" or "I wish I could do that"? No. First he developed an I CAN consciousness, followed by an I WILL determination. The result, as you know, was a groundbreaking enterprise that paved the way for other e-commerce businesses.

To create an I CAN awareness, burn those four letters "I C A N" into your mind. Avoid using the words *hope*, *wish* and *try*. Instead, emphasize the word CAN.

Every time you view the achievement of another, instead of quickly thinking, "I CAN'T," *know* that, if you wish, you can achieve the same thing. Even though, at the time, this may not seem exactly true to you, make the statement just the same. Soon you'll find that instead of closing with the negative feeling the task is beyond you, your mind will begin understanding how simple it will be to accomplish the deed.

## Create an I WILL Attitude.

This will help you overcome procrastination. As soon as you have an objective you know will help you reach a higher goal, get started on it at once. Do not put it off until the tomorrow that never comes. Many people have an I CAN awareness, but they never get beyond that. Instead, they make a list of excuses why they need to put off the start of something new.

Starting a task is usually the hardest part. Once it's underway, momentum takes over. In the beginning, you must first think of what you will do and how to do it. You have to consider the tools you'll need for the job, where they are and how to get them. After these steps are taken, a period of time passes before you get into full swing. You must spend time thinking about the job before getting started. This thinking stage may last for minutes, hours or even days. Sometimes the days extend into months and longer.

On one occasion, I was going to do a small job; then, for no good reason, I postponed it until the next day.

The next day, when my conscience began bothering me about the postponement, it dawned on me that if I'd done the job the day before, it would've been completed, and my mind would be free.

"Since time marches on," I thought, "why wouldn't it be better to dwell on the completed project rather than on one not yet started?" This way, your mind will think of the happy ending instead of the laborious beginning.

## Have a Definite Objective.

It's all very well to know you CAN do things—and WILL do things—but what do you intend to do? Know exactly what you want to accomplish to make your life more successful, happier and healthier. Then, you'll be ready for the next step.

## Develop a Do-It-Now Attitude.

After your objective has been analyzed and you find you CAN do it and WILL do it, the next step is to apply your do-it-now attitude, and DO it!

## *Unearthing Success in Your Mind*

Circumstances do not master you—you master them. If you aren't thrilled with your job, financial situation or life in general, change it. After all, you are the only one who can.

According to the *New York Times*, only 48.8 percent of businesses, started between 1977 and 2000, were still alive five years later. The same rate holds during both prosperous times and recessions.

There are numerous reasons for the great number of business failures, but my guess is many of the company heads who failed did so because they didn't start with a success consciousness. Most of them started in business with the *hope* they would make lots of money. The successful ones started by *knowing* they would make the grade.

Referring back to some of the principles we've already covered, recall that when you start anything with a success consciousness, you're guided to think the thoughts and do the things that will bring success.

When you're prompted by wishing, your subconscious mind guides you in thought and action to do the things that bring failure. Wishing is negative. Don't wish for the things you *know* you can get.

A salesperson selling ultrasound equipment said she worked really hard to sell one piece of equipment per week, the number she had to sell to make a fair living.

After attending a lecture devoted to success consciousness, she decided from that day forward, she would sell at least three ultrasound machines weekly. The next week she sold four and from then on, she averaged five and six per week. Today, she reports quite happily that she isn't working nearly as hard as she did before her revelation.

An advertising copywriter wrote good copy, but the writing was very difficult for him. He'd grind away for hours to produce something he'd consider just passable. Many times he rewrote an ad over and over before being satisfied.

Being in sales myself, this man asked me if there was anything he could do to lighten his workload. "Make your subconscious mind work for you," I suggested promptly.

At first he didn't understand my point, so I explained further. This man admitted he liked to write advertising copy, but he was actually afraid of it. He approached each assignment with the feeling it would be difficult, and it always proved to be.

"Build a success consciousness regarding your work," I explained. "If you begin building on the thought that you enjoy writing advertising copy, and it's a cinch for you to do, you'll notice a marked difference in your work."

In no time, this copywriter turned out twice as much copy as he had before, and it was far better material. "The thoughts flow as fast as I can put them down on paper," he declared.

To those who know anything at all about the workings of the mind, this is no miracle. If you hold a thought that a certain task will be difficult, your subconscious accepts the thought as an instruction and actually *makes* the task difficult.

If, on the other hand, you enjoy a certain job and know it'll prove to be easy for you, your subconscious mind accepts that thought as an instruction and guides you in doing your work quickly and well.

By now it should be clear you are what you think you are. If you haven't been getting as much out of life as you might have wished for, there's no one to blame but yourself.

## *Practice Makes Perfect*

Knowledge has value only when you make use of it. Practice the ideas we've covered so far, and give them a chance to work for you. Don't approach your practice wondering if they'll work. They work for others, and they will work for you.

This exercise is about you. You can practice as many different objectives as you want. You can begin developing a success consciousness about money, career or personal life. You can begin building an awareness that you can have great talent in any field you choose.

If your personality isn't the way you want it to be, begin developing a success consciousness to guide you to think the things and do the things that will make your personality magnetic.

Practice these new techniques until you begin seeing the changes you're after.

# Fifteen: Allowing Success

Nature always gives. It provides us with food, shelter, medicine, beauty and peace. Whatever we need, we can find it somewhere in nature. Why, then, do people feel so shorted by life? It may have something to do with the law of abundance.

The law of abundance states that the amount of worldly goods you're able to acquire is in direct proportion to the heights to which you increase your sights. In other words, if you can't see yourself having it, it will never come your way.

In America, it's been estimated that only 20 percent of the population holds 95 percent of the country's wealth. That means most of us are not in that select group, but it doesn't mean we can't get there. Now that you have a success mindset and are practicing the techniques in this book, you can develop the kind of *I WILL* determination that breaks through that threshold and allows you to join the select group of those holding this country's wealth.

In attempt to take advantage of the law of abundance by increasing your sights, you begin with the knowledge that the key to the quest lies within your own mind. How much you draw from the source of abundance depends entirely upon the success consciousness you've developed.

If what you want seems to be beyond the realm of possibility and you can't possibly imagine yourself possessing it, it'll do you little good to strive for it. The doubt in your mind will prevent you from achieving it.

The main idea in this module is to encourage you to have faith and believe in your own abilities. Many times what we think is faith is nothing but wishful thinking. We sincerely *try* to believe, but the long-established pattern of doubt in our minds breaks through and neutralizes the thoughts we hope will become beliefs.

## Fear of Success: The Hidden Enemy

Some people, for whatever reason, think they don't deserve success and happiness. It might be due to something in their upbringing, the current situation of their friends and family, or because they feel guilty about something in their past. Whatever the reason, some people actually fear success.

A friend of mine came from a family of successful attorneys and physicians, yet he struggled along in minimum-wage jobs. Delving into his situation, I found he had a fear of success. Why? Many of the successful people in his family had driven themselves so hard they found release in substance abuse.

Due to this, many of his family members crashed, burned and eventually ended up in rehab. One committed suicide and a few had ruined marriages. Is it any wonder he feared success? Finally, he was able to get his fear under control and finish his college degree. Now he has a fulfilling life as a college professor. He may not be the wealthiest person in the world, but he is definitely happier and more fulfilled.

Ask yourself if you have any anxieties or fears concerning success. Do you come from an upbringing that teaches you it's selfish to want material possessions and success for yourself? Do you have any deep feelings that you're unworthy in some way, whether from lack of education or the belief you're not intelligent or likeable enough to be successful? Do you have difficulty interacting socially with people? Does this make you feel inferior?

Turn any of these anxieties over to your subconscious mind to resolve. Lots of people have overcome these anxieties and have gone on to lead very successful lives.

You aren't helping anyone by arguing for your own limitations. Release your old mindset in order to revel in the abundance of the universe.

## *The Law of Abundance*

"I don't believe in that mind over matter stuff," a young man once told me. "Gurus or whatever claim that if you think a certain way, you're good to go. Success will grab you by the hand and stay with you the rest of your life."

Most people share this same skepticism. That's why the vast majority of people fail to succed in life.

"Do you consider yourself a success?" I asked this young man.

"No, I don't," he quickly replied.

"Why not?" I asked.

He gave lots of excuses. He'd had too little education. He didn't have any connections to help him better himself. He had no money and couldn't leave his job long enough to start a new career. On and on he went, giving no valid reasons for his failure.

The way this man talked about success, you'd think there wasn't enough of it to go around and that a large percentage of people were doomed to fail. I talked with him at length about the law of abundance. I pointed out that there was enough success for everyone, and that the more people who acquired success consciousness, the more there was for others.

Through a series of carefully thought-out questions, I led him on until he'd given a full list of reasons for his failures in life. Then, I went through these alibis one by one and proved they were not reasons, they were excuses. Finally, he began seeing there was a solid foundation to the idea of mind over matter. He not only thought of things he *could* do but things he *would* do.

## Testing the Abundance Law

In this life we crawl before we walk and walk before we run. This may be a good pattern to follow in testing the law of abundance. Test it first in a modest way. Perhaps you're driving an old car. Millions of new ones are made every year and are sold to millions of people. One of them might as well be yours.

Decide first that you intend to get a brand new car. Determine the make and model you want. Establish in your mind that you have the necessary faith to enable you to get it; next, put that faith into action. Before retiring at night, implant in your subconscious the idea that you'll be guided to think the thoughts and do the things to make the new car a reality.

This test should mean a lot to you. It should make you begin understanding that you *can* get what you want in life. If you operate with faith and not wishes, you'll be amazed to find how quickly you'll be driving your new car.

Go a step further in your next test, and further in the next. Until you have accomplished everything you set out to do, one step at a time.

There will never be any shortage of opportunity from the universe for you. The law of abundance is ever giving. Work according to the law, and it will work for you.

## *Letting It Happen*

Do you wonder if the work involved in getting what you want is really worth it? Many people worry the road to riches is so long and hard, they'll get stuck before they ever get started.

Suppose you received a large inheritance check and deposited it in the bank. Would you suddenly feel wealthy, even though you knew the money wouldn't be available for a few days? Of course you would, because you know the money will be available soon. The principles in this book may not have given you a check or a specific amount, but they are, in essence, a signed blank check. A check you may fill out for any amount you wish—any amount your beliefs can support.

It doesn't matter if the deposit has "cleared" the bank yet. If you believe it's on its way, you can begin to look and feel the part of a person of wealth. That attitude adjustment is another way you can build your fortune.

I was once told a story about a homeless man that illustrates this point perfectly. John once worked in a professional office but had fallen on bad times. After living on the streets for a few years, he made up his mind to get his life back together. First, he needed a job.

This former professional knew the importance of looking the part. With no money in his threadbare pockets, he walked into a small men's clothing store and asked to see the owner. Once he explained his situation, he asked the owner if there was any way they could strike a deal for a new suit. The owner agreed that John could help in the storeroom building shelves and unpacking merchandise to help pay for the new clothing.

A month after doing the odd jobs for the clothing-store owner, John returned to the store wearing his new suit. He delivered the news that he'd landed a job at a nearby office. He thanked the shop owner once again for his generosity and promised never to buy a suit from anyone but this small shop.

Today, John has a good job and makes it a point to buy several new suits every year from the shop owner. He also sends all of his colleagues to the man for their clothing.

Did John become a success because of the new suit? No. He became a success because he began seeing himself as one. Despite some poor choices in the past and a rough roadblock on his life's path, John envisioned a different future for himself. That changed his attitude, which gave others something in which to believe. John changed his own future by believing in himself.

## *Kicking Fear to the Curb*

I'm sure John was afraid to walk into that small shop and ask a stranger for help. I'm sure he was afraid to apply for that job, let alone go for an interview, but he did it anyway.

The unknown can be terrifying. Therefore, we worry so much—because we have no idea what to expect next.

This is especially true when you make the decision to go after a new life.

Maybe you think it's impossible to adopt the strategies in this book and change your own life because your problems are more difficult to solve than everyone else's. Everyone feels this way. Trust me when I tell you, that's the fear talking. Stop letting your problems dictate what you do and don't do. If you attempt to apply the success principles you've learned while your mind is fogged with problems, you won't gain a clear perspective of what you want to accomplish. As you try to hold a mental image of yourself as a prosperous individual, conflicting thoughts from the vague quarters of your mind will intrude, neutralizing the effect of your constructive thoughts. It's like trying to write while someone continually talks to you. You can't keep your mind on the subject matter and may subconsciously begin transcribing their message instead of your own.

One way to help stop the fear and develop a clear vision for yourself is to write down everything you're worried about or fearful of. This list of problems isn't intended to make you feel worse, but to give you a clear vision of the obstacles that must be overcome and a way to divert your attention from them to the job at hand.

Once you can focus your attention away from your worries and toward your goals, you can develop the success consciousness we have been discussing.

# Sixteen: The Benefits of a Positive Outlook

By now you've probably decided there are a few things you need to change about yourself to become the success you want to be. That is a good realization, but maybe you're now left wondering how to accomplish the change.

As we discussed in depth, the key to change is the way you think about yourself and the problem you want to solve. If you can think of these problems in a positive way, they will be quick and easy to resolve. Until you train your brain to naturally turn every negative into a positive, it's good practice to consciously focus positive energy toward the condition you wish to change.

## *Gaining Mastery over the Self*

Until you can master yourself, you'll never be able to master your environment. By environment I'm referring to your health, well-being and financial prosperity. Self-mastery is the condition in which your body is your servant, not your master.

If you find you're controlled by certain habits you'd like to overcome, instead of thinking of them as having enslaved you, hold a thought of self-mastery by knowing you have the power to overcome any unpleasant habits.

If laziness holds you back, learn to like the things you have to do instead of focusing on your resentment of them or skipping them altogether to solely focus on the things you *like* to do.

Here's an affirmation for developing self-mastery:

*Each time a negative thought attempts to enter my mind, I will immediately become aware of it and dissolve it with a positive thought. My self-confidence is increasing daily as I gain greater mastery over myself.*

What are some things holding you back that you need help mastering? Here are a few common obstacles I can help you with:

## Overcoming Shyness

A good formula to use in changing any condition is to concentrate on the condition you want to attain, not the condition you're attempting to overcome. Don't attempt this with thoughts such as:

*I will not be shy.*

This gives power to the existing condition. You don't want to be timid, so don't think about it. Instead, focus on a truly positive thought, such as:

*I like people. I like to be with people. I like to talk with people.*

Don't merely use lip service. As you affirm the fact you like people and like to talk to people, actually see yourself enjoying, not fearing, the company of others.

## Finding Your Mojo

What's a magnetic personality? Why is one person downright dazzling while others seem so dull? A person's mojo or personality isn't something you see but something you feel. The magnetism one projects to others comes from the heart.

It consists of love, friendliness, generosity, understanding and more. An individual's appearance doesn't actually dictate his or her level of attraction. Even the dullest-looking person can have the most mesmerizing personality that makes you want to spend time with them. Therefore, since personal magnetism is an intangible thing, something we project from within, it must be placed within the category of mind. This means that, if necessary or desirable, it can be changed by the mind.

As interesting as it may seem, when you hold to the thought—*I have a magnetic personality.*—you're literally guided to do the things that will give you a magnetic personality. You become friendly, generous, understanding. You *naturally* do all the things that attract others to you.

Along with your desire to like people, cultivate the habit of thinking of their comfort and happiness over your own. *Know* that due to your genuine interest in other people, your personality will grow more magnetic.

## Improving Your Mental Concentration

Today's society encourages having a low attention span. Multitasking is the norm. We're expected to be able to talk on the phone, read email and cook dinner all at the same time.

This multitasking carries over into our mental habits. We think of one thing, and then another thought enters our consciousness, and we forget about the first thing. Then, another thought creeps along, and another. By then, our concentration is completely derailed.

Mental concentration is our ability to hold on to one thought until we're through with it, before going to the next one. The value of mental concentration is so great it can rightfully be referred to as an art, yet it's so easy to acquire.

First of all, avoid such statements as, "I can't concentrate," "I'm so scatterbrained," or "I'm having a blond moment." These statements encourage the subconscious mind to maintain such a condition.

To develop the powers of concentration, try repeating this affirmation:

*I'm blessed with great powers of mental concentration. I can hold my thoughts on a single idea until I elect to let it go.*

## Building a Good Memory

Whenever you use the expressions "I've forgotten" or "I can't remember," you put the powers of mind to work against you. You know by now that your subconscious mind accepts such thoughts as instructions. In this case, it works toward giving you a bad memory. It sees to it that you did forget.

The subconscious is your memory storehouse. It retains everything you've heard, seen or read since your birth, right up to the present moment. To forget means you lack the ability to bring into consciousness information you already have in your subconscious. If you want to bring a fact into consciousness, and it doesn't come readily, instead of saying, "I have forgotten," say something like, "It will come to me in a moment," and it will.

So, from this moment on, think in terms of "I have a good memory." You'll be surprised to find your memory *is* good.

## Becoming a Good Conversationalist

It's easier than you think to acquire the art of conversation. Here are a few simple guidelines:

- Listen to what's being said before speaking. It gives you the opportunity to respond thoughtfully to the ideas presented by others.

- Include others in your conversation. If you see someone who's reluctant to talk, ask that person's opinion. Don't do it in a way that puts them on the spot or seems argumentative, but as a means of inviting them to participate and showing them their opinion is valuable. This will make others more inclined to talk to you. No one likes it when one person dominates the conversation.

- Be enthusiastic about your subject. People will be much more likely to listen to you if you're excited about what you say. Show self-confidence.

- Smile. It gives the impression you care about others, and they'll feel more engaged in what you say.

Give the suggestion to your subconscious that you wish to become a good conversationalist. It will take over from there. Say, "I am a good conversationalist." Say it many, many times, and practice!

## Learning to Relax

I hear so many people say they have trouble relaxing. Some even claim they're incapable. When I hear that, I know they speak the truth because the "can't relax" thought acts as an instruction to the subconscious mind, which in turn maintains the tension in the person who said it. When you're tense, you burn energy. When you're relaxed, you store energy.

Develop a relaxation consciousness. Know you can relax. A person who is fully relaxed loses body consciousness. They aren't aware of their legs, arms and body and are almost like a mind afloat.

Practice relaxation. Learn to sit down and feel a looseness throughout your entire body. Ten minutes of this relaxation will do you a lot of good since short periods of relaxed rest are more beneficial than longer periods when the body is tense.

Cats are great examples of master relaxers. They will look very tired, yawn a couple of times and drop off into peaceful sleep. In just a few minutes, they'll wake completely relaxed and ready for a hunt. That's the benefit and power of relaxation.

Remember to accentuate the positive as far as relaxation is concerned. Until you master the art of relaxation, give your mind frequent instructions, such as:

*I am the master of my being and can fully relax at will. My mind is dwelling on peaceful, harmonious thoughts.*

## Building Self-Confidence

Just as you enjoy being with people who have self-confidence, so too will others enjoy being with you when you reflect that same quality. The real meaning of self-confidence is balance. We think of the individual who can keep him- or herself under control under all conditions as showing self-confidence.

Thomas Jefferson said, "Nothing gives one person so much advantage over another as to remain always cool and unruffled under all circumstances."

A self-confident person possesses these desirable characteristics:

- control
- sound reasoning
- good judgment
- sincerity
- vanity-free pride

- resistance to temptation

- faith in him- or herself

- ambition

Accentuate the positive. Constantly *see* yourself as possessing all the attributes that give you the self-confidence so admired by others.

# Seventeen: Mental Motivation

You've learned a lot of skills so far regarding how to change the way you think and what to do to turn your life around and accomplish great goals. However, there's one thing you must do to get started on this new journey. Get motivated. Until you're truly ready to start this new adventure, your efforts will be halfhearted and you will likely fail.

Motivation is the key to a successful outcome and begins by setting a purposeful path for yourself. Without a map to follow, your efforts won't amount to much. Yes, a positive outlook and the belief you can succeed are integral parts to your future success, but so is having a plan.

Success takes time, effort and planning. Every journey begins with a single step and continues inch by inch until the end is reached. The same is true for your journey toward prosperity. You will become successful by believing in yourself, getting motivated and then getting to work! You've already taken the first important steps; now let's set some goals so you know where you're headed.

## *Planning for Prosperity*

Begin by writing out your ultimate end goal. This is will be your perfect "dream." Be as specific as you can. You've already thought about what you want to accomplish in the next year, four years or 10 years. Now, write down those dreams. Maybe your ultimate goal is to make $5 million in the next 10 years by running your own publishing company. It's a hefty goal, but one you can accomplish.

# Designing Your Life

To use our one-step-at-a-time approach, let's take that big goal and think of 10 smaller goals you need to accomplish first. Your list may look similar to this:

Year 1: Begin writing a column for a major magazine.

Year 2: Write and publish first book.

Year 3: Open an e-book publishing company.

Year 4: Find two to four authors to begin writing e-books for your new company.

Year 5: Publish 10 new titles this year.

Year 6: Publish your first author's book.

Year 7: Find an investor to help finance the expansion of your company.

Year 8: Buy or start a small local newspaper.

Year 9: Expand into other publishing arenas.

Year 10: Sell your budding company or go public on the stock exchange in order to generate $5 million in profits that year.

Keep in mind this is only a sampling of the things you may decide to do to grow your business. The key here is to find intermediary goals designed to help you make your way toward obtaining your ultimate final goal.

Next, you must take these smaller goals and break them down into individual action steps. In the scenario above, you're giving yourself a one-year deadline to meet each goal. This means doing a lot of hard work in a short period of time, including figuring out how each of the business aspects of the individual goals works, etc.

For instance, in year one, your goal is to begin writing a column for a national magazine. First, you must learn how the publishing world works, how to write a winning column, and how to pitch and sell your idea — all within one short year. The purpose of this initial goal is to help you learn how the publishing world works and begin building a network within the industry.

Take each of your mini goals and plan out a list of specific action points that must be accomplished to meet your main goal for the term. These action points may then be broken down even further into monthly, weekly or daily tasks, keeping in mind each task, action point and goal all lead you on the path toward ultimate success. Each must build on the other in a way that helps propel you toward your final dream.

Laying out such a detailed plan may seem overwhelming, and it can be for some people. If trying to plan out the next 10 years seems too difficult, simply start with your first goal. Break it down into doable action points and tasks, assigning a deadline to each until this kind of approach becomes second nature. As you move through your list, it'll become easier and easier to see the steps that must be added so you can keep moving forward.

Sticking to the plan is good in the sense that it keeps you motivated and gives you a map to follow. However, sometimes taking an unexpected turn can actually allow you to travel in a new, different direction and may actually help propel you even further and faster. Never get so stuck on following your preplanned path that you don't try something new or even miss an opportunity that may actually benefit you the most.

## *Getting to Work*

You plan out a strategy for your success, but until you dig in and get to work, you'll never experience success or riches. Generating wealth takes long hours of hard work. By now you have a dream. You've created a vision and you've outlined a plan. All that's left is taking action. Begin with step one on your master plan and get to work. Success is yours—if you're not afraid to do the work necessary to achieve it.

# Eighteen:
# Enjoying a Life of Abundance

One day, a woman who loved boats and was adept at reading blueprints and using tools decided to build a boat of her own. She sent away for complete plans and specifications for a small cabin cruiser and dreamed of the day when, sitting behind the wheel, she'd guide the boat around the inland waters.

It's been several years since she purchased the plans, yet to this day, the keel has not been laid. She often gets out the plans and studies them, and then carefully folds and places them on a shelf in her den.

You now have the plans for a new life of health, wealth and happiness. You can put them away with the intention you'll make a start someday—which is not actually a date—or you can get started right now.

You'd be impatient with a builder who, when given a contract, visits the worksite, studies the blueprints, and then goes home to think about something else. A good builder, one who gets lots of work and recommendations, is one who assembles his materials and goes to work after the contract is signed.

Reading this book has been like signing a contract with yourself to build a better life, one that will give you pride as your friends and relatives praise you for your accomplishments. As a builder will read and reread the plans to make certain they're clear to him, you should reread this book. And then—you should get started.

Put this program aside for a day or two to digest it properly. Then, with determination, reread the entire book from the first page to the last, knowing you're shaping a life that will bring you all of the success and prosperity you may have dreamed about, but never expected to have.

Many of you, from the first reading, are already on your way. You've already started practicing the principles and are enjoying results. You'll reach great heights—of that I'm certain.

## Continue Practicing the Subconscious Mind

After you attain your goal, don't lose sight of the source of your good fortune. A trainer can help a person gain optimal health through proper exercise and diet. However, if, after becoming healthy, this person slips back into his or her former method of living, their physical being will slip back to its former unhealthy state.

Nothing stands still. It either goes forward or backward. As far as your thinking is concerned, you either continue to develop in the direction of positive thinking, or you slip back into the customary channels of negative thinking.

Since many people lean, to some degree, to the negative side, it's inevitable that most of the people we meet will be more negative than positive. Often, even after seeing the effect that positive thinking can have over their lives, these individuals fall right back into their old habits and undo what good they've done.

Most of the arguments presented by the negative-minded person about why conditions are bad, why it's hard to do this and that, why, under existing circumstances, it's not possible to succeed, seem logical. Under these conditions it's not hard for the one recently initiated into the realm of positive thinking to fall back in line with the great majority of negative thinkers.

I have a friend who invested $1,000 in an insurance business and built it up to a personal fortune of over $100,000,000. I'm sure that during his building years, many negative situations came to his attention. He was probably told many times about the things that could not be done, or why some of his employees were not able to close sales. Do you suppose he succumbed to the negative thoughts and relaxed his efforts? Not for a minute! He analyzed the problem to learn what prompted the negative thoughts, and then created plans for correcting the condition. That man will tell you in no uncertain terms that his positive mental attitude is wholly responsible for his great success.

Remember, there always has been, and probably always will be, a large majority of negative thinkers. This is why so comparatively few people ever reach the top. The principles included in this book can raise you to new heights. However, reading and applying the principles isn't an assurance you'll remain there. Unless you continue replacing negative thoughts with positive ones, it can be very easy to retrace your steps back to where you were before initiation into the fraternity of positive thinkers. You must reach the point where it becomes automatic for you to offset every negative with a positive.

## *Think about Your Future*

Throughout this book there were several repetitions to fix the truth more firmly in your consciousness. Now, let's think about your future. Let's lay out a routine for you to follow to assure that journey will ever be onward and upward.

1. **Never permit a negative thought to remain in your mind.** Immediately offset it with a positive one. If necessary, to eliminate the negative, do something positive to assure yourself the negative has disappeared.

2. **Always go to bed with positive thoughts.** Decide on the things you have to do the following day and go to bed with the positive thought that during the night, your subconscious mind will work with you.

The following day, you'll be guided to do your work effectively and with enthusiasm, having already worked out the kinks in your sleep.

3. **Keep your mind happy.** It's far easier to keep a happy mind positive than to transform one filled with gloom and sorrow. If gloom persists, do something to make someone else happy, and your happiness will resume.

4. **Start your day with enthusiasm.** As you awaken, be excited in anticipation of another day of progress and happiness. Know that, throughout the day, you'll be guided in thought and action to success in anything you attempt to do.

   At breakfast, talk about your happiness and enthusiasm and how you know it'll be a great day. If, by chance, you're with people who have not yet learned the power that comes from positive thinking, you can be happy you have a positive mind. On the other hand, if you spend time with a real go-getter, you will leave feeling like doing things and going places.

If at all possible, refrain from associating with negative people, unless it's a positive experience for you to help teach them how to gain the power that comes from a positive mind. If circumstances make it necessary for you to be in a negative atmosphere, stay happy with the thought you've conditioned your mind to be positive—in other words, enjoy the contrast.

5. **Move forward, not back.** As I said before, nothing stands still. It either goes forward or backward. "Every day, I'm on my way" is a motto I keep in a conspicuous spot in my home to help remind me to always move forward.

See to it that not a day passes without some progress. Until it becomes automatic for you to do so, you must make a conscious effort to take a progressive step each day. In time, and not long either, prosperity will come into your life and there will be no letup on progress.

Congratulations! You're now on your way to designing a whole new life, attracting exactly what you want and prospering along the way. But, don't stop when you reach your goal. There's always a new adventure to try. You now know the sky's the limit, so shoot for the stars. Life is an amazing adventure. Get out there and enjoy it!

# About the Author

Dennis M. Postema, RFC, is a successful entrepreneur, bestselling author, coach, speaker and registered financial consultant. He is also the founder of MotivationandSuccess.com, StoriesofPerseverance.org, FinancingYourLife.com and TheRetirementInstitute.org.

Over the past 12 years, Dennis has taught clients, agents and associates how to find motivation and ascend psychological barriers to achieve success. His dedication to improving lives has led him to work with renowned motivational and self-help industry heavyweights, such as Jack Canfield and Brian Tracy.

Dennis' personal experience with tragedy, life-changing surgeries and health issues has given him a unique perspective on what it means to achieve success and what's really standing in the way of it. He channels that perspective into educational and motivational books and programs in the topics of finance, perseverance, success and business.

His focus on helping clients, rather than simply selling products, landed him on the cover of *Agents Sales Journal (Senior Market Edition)* in 2011. In 2012, he was a recipient of the 10 Under 40 Award given by the Defiance Chamber of Commerce. He was also awarded the 2013 Distinguished Alumni Award from his alma mater, Northwest State Community College, for his success in the industry and community. His contribution to Jack Canfield's book, *Dare to Succeed*, earned him an Editor's Choice award.

## DESIGNING YOUR LIFE

What would happen if you discovered you could do more than just live your life—you could *design* it? This book teaches you to harness the power of your subconscious and program it to help you live a happy life fitting your definition of perfection.

## DESIGNING YOUR LIFE: ACTION GUIDE

These exercises help you master your subconscious, abolish negativity and raise self-esteem. This guide focuses on creative visualization and powerful affirmations to control your life's design and master your future.

## DEVELOPING PERSEVERANCE

A combination of internal roadblocks are holding you back, preventing you from persevering. This book shows you how to break through these self-imposed obstacles to begin moving along your true path, taking you further than you ever thought possible.

## DEVELOPING PERSEVERANCE: ACTION GUIDE

With this guide, you'll learn about the unique roadblocks you've designed for yourself and explore the thoughts, feelings and events that impact your ability to succeed.

## YOU DESERVE TO BE RICH

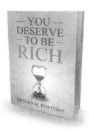

If you're busy blaming your lack of wealth on upbringing, education and environment, you're missing out on learning how easy it is to get rich. This book teaches you to throw away the excuses and focus on the 12 steps to securing a future of financial success.

## YOU DESERVE TO BE RICH: ACTION GUIDE

You deserve an ideal life. This workbook helps you get there by providing activities and strategies that explain the rules of greatness, help define your dreams and work to banish your fears.

## UNLEASH YOUR MOJO

You already possess everything you need to be the person you want to be, you just have to access these powerful traits. In *Unleash Your Mojo*, you'll learn to recognize all the greatness inside you and discover how to put it to use and start living your ideal life.

## UNLEASH YOUR MOJO: ACTION GUIDE

Each of us has power to succeed yet many of us never tap into that power. Instead we stagnate on the sidelines while others flash forward in life. This workbook gives practical tips, advice and exercises to advance in your quest for authenticity and power.

### THE POSITIVE EDGE

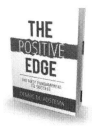

There's a secret behind living a happy, successful, fulfilling life: *positivity.* Learn how to overcome your tendency toward negativity, how to control your life and future, and how easy it is to improve your confidence and self-esteem.

### SPARK: THE KEY TO IGNITING RADICAL CHANGE IN YOUR BUSINESS

A complete, step-by-step training program to help you become a high performer and higher earner. Learn how to rise to the top of your profession, position yourself as an expert and attract the abundance you desire.

### DARE TO SUCCEED

Get motivation and information to rise to the next level of success! America's #1 Success Coach, Jack Canfield, has gathered together the top business minds in one powerful book. This guide holds their strategies to conquering the competition and creating ongoing abundance.

### VICTORY JOURNAL

The *Victory Journal* demonstrates the importance of writing down all your daily wins. Inside you'll find exercises to help define your ideal self and create action steps to move closer to your goals.

## HARNESSING THE POWER OF GRATITUDE

Recognize the positive energy moving through your day and harness it with this undated journal. Filled with inspirational quotes to help you maintain the spirit of gratitude, it's an ideal tool for developing an enduring, powerful habit of thankfulness.

## APPRECIATING ALL THAT YOU HAVE

This 365-day journal filled with inspirational quotes provides a safe space to write down the many things you're thankful for. It's the perfect way to help shift your perspective and recognize the abundance of positive forces in your life.

## THE PSYCHOLOGY OF SALES: FROM AVERAGE TO RAINMAKER

Take your sales from lackluster to rainmaker without any smarm, aggressive tactics or dishonesty. This book teaches sales pros the psychology of their customers so they can present products the right way for each shopper.

## THE PSYCHOLOGY OF SALES: ACTION GUIDE

In this action guide, you'll gain greater insight into your own personality and psychological makeup as well as that of your customers so you can further your sales success and transform your career.

## RETIREMENT YOU CAN'T OUTLIVE

Cut through the hype and challenge conventional wisdom with a book focusing on conservative and reasonable ways to save for retirement. This book uses plain language and lots of common sense that's been missing from financial planning sessions for decades.

## RETIREMENT YOU CAN'T OUTLIVE: ACTION GUIDE

Transform the lessons taught in *Retirement You Can't Outlive* into action steps that change the shape of your financial future. This immersive tool contains worksheets, exercises and review sheets to help you develop a plan to rescue your financial future.

## NAVIGATING THROUGH MEDICARE

Don't be confused by the rules, plans and parts of Medicare. This book simplifies the complex system and allows you to quickly and easily make the right decision for the future of your healthcare. It's a one-stop guide to everything you need to know.

## AVOIDING A LEGACY NIGHTMARE

Poor planning can rip your estate from your loved ones. *Avoiding a Legacy Nightmare* is a simple guide to help you get started in creating an effective estate plan that achieves all that you intended.

### PHYSICIANS: MONEY FOR LIFE

If you want to retire on your own terms, you must understand the special considerations that physicians need to make in order to maintain sustainable retirement plans. *Physicians: Money for Life* casts aside traditional advice that's not suited to conservative retirement planning and focuses on helping physicians design a plan that creates money for life.

### PHYSICIANS: MONEY FOR LIFE: ACTION GUIDE

You have the knowledge necessary to change the financial health of your retirement, now it's time to apply it. This action guide helps you transform the lessons taught in *Physicians: Money for Life* into action steps you can take to change the shape of your retirement.

With worksheets, exercises and review, this guide will help you move forward in your retirement planning journey while devising a plan to save it.

### ALZHEIMER'S LEGACY GUIDE

Alzheimer's patients and their caregivers face a race against the clock and must learn how to cement a well-thought-out legacy plan before the disease's mental, emotional and psychological effects start to take their toll. This book provides guidance to both the recently diagnosed and those who will care for them as the disease progresses.

## FINANCING YOUR LIFE: THE STORY OF FOUR FAMILIES

This is the story of four families that took their financial lives out of the red and into the black. There's McKenna, a single mom of two boys, working hard every day as a waitress; Toby and Shannon, two professionals battling a layoff and personal spending demons; Blake and Christine, a newlywed couple in a hurry to start living the good life, whether they can afford it or not; and Marcie and Kurt, two young parents struggling to keep up in an increasingly image-obsessed society.

## FINANCING YOUR LIFE: THE FINANCIAL RECOVERY KIT

Financing Your Life is an innovative financial recovery kit devoted to teaching you how to take total control over your financial life. Within, you'll learn about the secret behind financial planning, budgeting basics, insurance, credit repair, getting out of debt, developing financial compromise with a spouse or partner, saving and investing, mortgages and more. This tool does more than just tell you about financial concepts; it helps you begin immediately integrating what you learn into your own financial life. This tool does more than just tell you about financial concepts; it helps you begin immediately integrating what you learn into your own financial life.